PLANNING YOUR *Wedding* SUCKS

What to do when
place cards, plus ones, and
paying two grand for a cake
make you miserable

JOANNE KIMES *&* ELENA DONOVAN MAUER

Adams media

Avon Massachusetts

Published by
Adams Media, a division of F+W Media, Inc.
57 Littlefield Street, Avon, MA 02322. U.S.A.
www.adamsmedia.com

ISBN 10: 1-4405-0203-X
ISBN 13: 978-1-4405-0203-3
eISBN 10: 1-4405-0910-7
eISBN 13: 978-1-4405-0910-0

Printed in the United States of America.

10   9   8   7   6   5   4   3   2   1

Library of Congress Cataloging-in-Publication Data

Kimes, Joanne.
Planning your wedding sucks / Joanne Kimes and Elena Donovan Mauer.
p. cm.
Includes index.
ISBN-13: 978-1-4405-0203-3
ISBN-10: 1-4405-0203-X
ISBN-13: 978-1-4405-0910-0 (ebk)
ISBN-10: 1-4405-0910-7 (ebk)
1. Weddings—Planning. 2. Wedding etiquette. I. Mauer, Elena Donovan.
II. Title.
HQ745.K456 2010
395.2'2—dc22
2010038807

Note paper © istockphoto.com/evigen

This book is available at quantity discounts for bulk purchases.
For information, please call 1-800-289-0963.

Dedication

To every woman who's always thought being engaged would be magical when sometimes, it's pretty damn awful. And to everyone who's been accused of being a diva, a Bridezilla, a cheapskate, a Little Miss Picky, a vacant fiancée, or a not-quite-good-enough soon-to-be daughter-in-law—and was really just trying to make herself, and everyone else she knows and loves, happy for one sweet day.

Other Books in the Sucks *Series*

Bedtime Sucks

Breastfeeding Sucks

Christmas Sucks

Divorce Sucks

Grammar Sucks

Menopause Sucks

Potty Training Sucks

Pregnancy Sucks

Pregnancy Sucks for Men

Teenagers Suck

Acknowledgments

Many thanks to brilliant agent Molly Lyons, whip-smart editor Meredith O'Hayre, and writing partner Joanne Kimes. Without you wonderful ladies, this book would not exist and plenty of engaged women would be left wondering why they're stress-eating when they're supposed to be on cloud nine.

I also would like to mention the amazing magazine and web editors and writers who taught me everything I know about writing about the bridal industry—you all know who you are! But really, I wouldn't have a clue about what brides want to know without the hundreds of real women who, over the years, let me interview them, answered my questionnaires and Facebook posts, and vented to me about wedding planning over Pinot Grigio. Your feedback and stories were inspiration for every page of this book (and yup, some of it is actually quoted—gold stars to those peeps!).

I, of course, have to thank my husband Anthony for suggesting we get married (and following through with it). Engagement and marriage have, at times, made me want to pull out my hair, but being with you every day makes it all worth it. Thank you also to Ryan—if you weren't such a good baby, I would have never gotten this thing written. You both make me laugh every day.

Contents

Introduction

Congratulations, you're engaged! You can now look down at your ring finger and see an actual diamond instead of an empty patch of skin where you once dreamed some bling would someday live. Whether it's a result of love at first sight or an ultimatum (I'm just being realistic here), you finally got your man to propose! I hope it was a romantic story that you'll share with your grandkids, like something that you'd see in a Reese Witherspoon movie, where your guy picked an ultra-romantic location and a fabulous Tiffany setting. But even if he popped the question in full face paint after his team won the big game, you still have the man, the ring, and "Here Comes the Bride" stuck in your head. You've made the important leap from "girlfriend" to "fiancée" and I encourage you to enjoy the elation while it lasts.

Now back to reality. Once your guy gets up from bended knee and the reality of planning the wedding sets in, it's all downhill. There's a whole yellow snowball of stress coming your way and it could get out of control pretty damn fast. The stress can come in many forms: the so-called compliments your former sorority sisters make about your "so-little-it's-adorable!" diamond, the newfound battles you and your fiancé have over everything from the guest list (former friends with benefits need not RSVP) to the wine list (I don't care if his mother drinks Arbor Mist, she can live with chardonnay for the day), the caterer who promises you filet but delivers Hamburger Helper, your mother's hissy fit because you want to buy a new dress instead of wearing what could only be called her "wedding muu-muu," and, well, just about everything else!

But fortunately, that's where this book comes in. For the last eight years, I've been writing for and editing bridal publications, and I've learned quite a bit about planning a wedding without name calling or runaway brides. But unlike the magazines and books that make planning a bash that looks like it sprung from the pages of *Martha Stewart* look easy, I don't promise that your wedding planning will be stress free. Even I, a so-called "expert," had my own setbacks and tribulations. After planning my dream wedding, my husband got "called up" by the military reserves—he was being sent to the Middle East for an indefinite amount of time. We quickly cancelled everything and got hitched at City Hall two days later. When Mr. Wonderful came home, I pulled together a more conventional bash—with its share of complexities—in just a few months. As a result, I know a thing or two about losing deposits, making compromises, the bridesmaid from hell, and big day emergencies. Honestly, planning your wedding can suck. But with the tips in this book, and several cocktails along the way, it will suck a whole lot less.

Chapter 1

You're Engaged!
(It's All Downhill from Here)

I've heard this many times: "I'm engaged. Now what?" In fact, I once got an e-mail from a relative in another state telling me that her daughter was engaged and asking me to e-mail her back and tell her everything she needed to know. What I wanted to say was, "Um . . . I've written about wedding planning for the better part of a decade now—spent my 9-to-5 on this stuff day in and day out. There are entire magazines that come out monthly and websites that are updated daily with information about planning a wedding. And you want me to sum it up in an e-mail . . . really?! If I thought that was actually possible, I would have written that e-mail years ago, had it published, and then twiddled my thumbs while collecting paychecks!" (But I didn't say that.) My point here is this: There's a lot to do: a lot of researching and a lot to take into consideration. Knowing where to start is not exactly self-explanatory.

So here's the fit-in-an-e-mail version of your first three steps:

1. Form a "vision" for your wedding.
2. Set your budget and decide how you'll spend it.
3. Find the right help to get all this crap done.

Do nothing else until you've done these three things. Here's how.

JACKIE AND JOHN OR COURTNEY AND KURT?

In general, there are two kinds of brides: those who have fantasized about Chantilly lace and fondant icing since they were little girls, and those who rarely gave their wedding day a second thought. No matter which camp you belong to, your first step in wedding planning is to decide what it is you want from your wedding day. And I mean today, as a grown adult. A lot has changed since you walked Barbie and Ken down the aisle, except for the fact that a pink Corvette and a Malibu beach house are still killer additions to any marriage.

It's important to have a distinct vision of your wedding day before you start the planning process because once you set foot in a dress salon or florist's studio, you'll be bombarded with choices. And without the vision to direct you, you could easily become overwhelmed, confused, or rushed into spending money on something that turns out to be not-quite-right. And while it's okay to, say, browse casually to get some ideas, it's not okay to buy anything or—I really mean this one—go to one of those crazy bridal shows until you've created your vision. To get started, ask yourself some probing questions:

- What have I dreamed the day would be like?
- In what type of setting would I like to have the ceremony and reception?
- Who would I like to have there to celebrate with my fiancé and me?
- What style and feel would I like the day to have?
- What are my top three priorities for my wedding day?

Answering these questions will give you a clear jumping off point. Remember that everything about your wedding day will stem from your location, the size of the guest list, and any sort of theme or style choices you've made. So those choices are what will guide you as you make all those tough decisions. Think of it as planning a kids birthday party, except without paper plates and scary clowns (believe me, your Uncle Leo dancing the Macarena will be scary enough). Find your focus.

While thinking about these major decisions, don't neglect to run them by your fiancé. You know, the dude that used to be the main focus of your life that will soon be pushed aside in favor of choosing invitation fonts and veil lengths? Yeah, that guy. You may be marrying a man who wants to sit back and let you decide it all (or is too afraid to voice his opinion and set you off), or he may state his opinion loud and clear and it may be the direct opposite of yours. Either way, you'll want to save yourself future bickering—or passive-aggressive helping-out boycotts—by asking him for his thoughts up front. Find out what your guy thinks the big day should be like and hope to high heaven that you two have roughly the same sort of picture in mind.

Now here's a for instance: Maybe you're envisioning a small refined gathering with the two of you exchanging vows on a cliff top in Hawaii and dining on a seafood platter buffet. Your guy? He wants 200 of his closest friends and family (with their small children, of course!), an outdoor Western motif, and a taco bar reception. While you're tempted to backpedal on the whole wedding deal or deny him sex to get your way (wait, that comes after a few years of marriage), remember that this day is about the two of you and it should reflect both of your personalities and wishes. Plus, this is the first of many compromises you'll have to make throughout your marriage, so you best learn how to start being flexible now. Maybe Hawaii is too far, but there's a cliff overlooking a nearby lake where you could have the ceremony, and then have seafood tacos for a reception of only 100 guests. Or perhaps you head to Hawaii, but you bring a crew of friends and relatives along with you (with their kids) and marry in a Hawaiian church, with a cocktail hour on that cliff. See, there are some compromises that actually sound pretty cool.

WHAT? IT'S NOT ALL ABOUT ME?

Now, if trying to "compromise" only results in screaming matches, take a step back. Think about your relationship. Is this really how you're going to approach the big decisions in life? If your guy is totally inflexible, think about why he wants to have this wedding his way only. Is it because this is his first wedding and your second? Is he stubborn or controlling? Does one of you really deserve more say than the other? Is it an unequal partnership? I didn't think so.

I cried like a big, fat baby when my now-husband suggested getting married at City Hall. What about the big church wedding I'd been fantasizing about? What about the professional photographer? My dad walking me down the aisle? All those wonderful, sentimental, and expensive things? I'm pretty lucky, because he let me cry about that stuff without pointing out that what I should be crying about was his going to war. Once I pulled my ridiculous self together, I realized what was important—and that was that we wanted to vow to spend our lives together. So my next step was to pick up the phone, call our close friends and family, and invite them to City Hall two days later.

"Ian proposed in Rome after seeing the Sistine Chapel. He told me he initially was going to do it the night before, over dinner, but when my meal arrived, the pasta was shaped like little penises. I guess he didn't want to associate his proposal with a tiny wiener."

—Erica

My point is, wedding dreams are usually just that: dreams. And while they're wonderful and oftentimes meaningful (family traditions and religions do come into play), they're certainly not worth risking your relationship for. You can't merge your two different visions? Decide that neither of you "wins" and come up with a completely new wedding idea together. Listen, if you can't agree on this, how are you going to agree on things during your married life?

Once you and your man have "the talk" and find your compromise, together you'll have created a vision for your wedding day. Now, I don't promise to be a miracle worker—*everything* about this wedding vision may not come true (more on that in the next section). However, by envisioning the dream wedding and coming up with some priorities, you've created a focus for your event. And with focus, wading through the thousands of ideas that will come at you will suck a lot less. You'll have inspiration and be able to easily eliminate the not-quite-right choices. Focus will prevent you from getting sidetracked or from breaking out in stress-induced hives.

A GUIDE FOR THE PLANNING PERPLEXED

Setting an overall theme for your wedding can be overwhelming. But what it comes right down to is your (and your mate's) personality. Here are some basic themes to start you thinking:

Romantic: If you have flowery elegance in mind, picture this: A ceremony and reception in a hotel ballroom, historic home or somewhere else with opulent chandeliers, ornate fireplaces, and grand staircases. Keep it intimate by inviting your 60 nearest and dearest and decorate with red roses. For dessert? Red velvet cake.

Rock 'n' Roll: Maybe you and your fiancé are really into music. Choose an excellent band that can work with you to create an awesome set list that's not only rife with your favorite songs but will also get guests rockin' on the dance floor. Maybe you don't spend lots of loot on an indulgent dinner but instead, give every guest a backstage pass to an amped up cocktail reception.

Preppy: Are you more Jackie and John than Courtney and Kurt? Picture a New England-style country club wedding. Crisp linens in navy and white can decorate your space. During the cocktail hour, serve lobster rolls and entertain your guests with a swing band.

Sporty: Do you both root for the same team? Imagine entering your reception to the tune of the Monday Night Football theme. Instead of numbering the tables, name each table after a different player on your favorite team. Have the groom's cake shaped to resemble his alma mater's stadium.

These are only a handful of ideas. You could go Disco, Roaring Twenties, Formal, Asian, Klingon . . . the sky's the limit. Your tastes and interests will dictate countless others.

SIZE MATTERS . . . OR AT LEAST THE SIZE OF YOUR BUDGET

Ah, money—it's usually the thing that sucks the most about wedding planning. In fact, I'm sure the person who quipped, "Money is the root of all evil," must have done so while planning a wedding. Everything about money sucks: budgeting, overspending, saving—basically the whole financial enchilada. The only thing that doesn't suck about money is the prospect of having so much of it you could swim and take nose dives in it like Uncle Scrooge does. (Yes, I referenced Duck Tales. So what?) Unless you're like Star Jones and can get your wedding stuff for free by promoting the vendors on The View, you need to create a wedding budget. Whether it's

$1,000 or $100,000, a wedding budget is vitally important because it will keep you from overspending, help you prioritize, and essentially keep everything in perspective—and in check. Big or small, your budget starts with a number. Here's how you find yours.

First, figure out where all the money for your wedding will be coming from. How much do you and your fiancé have saved up? How much will your parents and/or his parents contribute? You should be very clear from the get go exactly how much you have to work with. There are two reasons for this: one is that asking someone to pay for, say, the flowers can be misinterpreted as letting them *choose* the flowers. And you really want your wedding flowers to be lilacs, not the wilted carnations that your future mother-in-law can get for half price. The other reason is that if you've already committed to something and your loved ones can't or won't pay for it, you might get stuck having paid a nonrefundable deposit or, worse, laying out money on a credit card that you won't be able to repay.

Now, allow me to take this opportunity to very, very strongly suggest that you do *not* use a credit card to pay for your wedding. The only way you should ever use a credit card is if you already have the money to pay the full balance at the end of the month *and* you're getting some great rewards points for purchases you make (plane tickets for your honeymoon perhaps?). Otherwise, despite any plans you have to get that big promotion at work or win the Power Ball, you will be paying for this wedding for years. And if you think fighting about wedding planning is fun, just wait until after you're married and start fighting about your debt. Good times! Plus, you risk screwing up your credit, which is no way to enter the state of wedlock. If you want to purchase a house or car in the future, you'll be in deep doo-doo if you have bad credit.

MONEY MISTAKES

- **Mistake #1:** Forgetting to give yourself a "cushion." Wedding spending almost always goes over budget. Make sure you pad your budget about 5 to 10 percent just in case you happen to come across a pricey dress you have to have or, say, you need to pay extra to put a rush on your invitations. This almost always happens.
- **Mistake #2:** Not keeping track of the small stuff. A unity candle here. A gift for a bridesmaid there. All those little things don't seem to cost too much on their own, but they really add up. Whenever you make a purchase, big or small, be sure to subtract it from your budget. Otherwise you're liable to find yourself wondering where the hell all the money went.
- **Mistake #3:** Neglecting your wedding focus. It's easy to want the best of the best for everything about your wedding. But remember: no one can have it all, except maybe Tori Spelling, whose dad paid for her first wedding (and look how that one turned out). So if you are going nuts to rent out a lavish venue, remember to cut back on some other things to make up for it. Be realistic. If the location is beautiful, you probably don't need oodles of imported flowers.
- **Mistake #4:** Not taking contributions seriously. Your parents offer you some money for your wedding but then you go over budget, expecting them to give you more. Isn't that presumptuous and disrespectful? Show your appreciation by taking the 'rents' moolah

and making the most of it. Stretch those buckaroos. You don't want to fight about funds and get disowned well before your dad walks you down the aisle.

Who Pays for What?

Just as there are different wedding themes, there are different ways to pay for them. Here are the most common:

Keeping with Tradition. Back before important inventions like the polio vaccine and ceramic flattening irons, the bride's family was expected to pay for the wedding. Those days are long gone. Sure, if your folks are super generous, take them up on it. But don't count your chicken dinners before they're hatched. Also, if keeping with tradition, make sure your future in-laws are cool with springing for the rehearsal dinner.

Mr. and Ms. Independent. For professional couples, a great way to pay for your wedding is to, um, pay for your wedding. Yes, yourselves. All of it. If you're not privy to any financial help, this will have less to do with independence and more to do with desperation. Either way, there is a *huge* benefit to paying your own way: you have complete and total control over all your wedding decisions, and that can be worth its weight in gold (probably only 10 karat though, since you'll be footing the bill).

Even Steven. A common way to pay for a wedding today is to split the total budget three equal ways: between you and your fiancé, your parents, and your in-laws. Each party pays their equal share. This is especially effective if both families are eager and able to help out and you're able to commit to a specific dollar amount right off the bat. It's not necessarily a good choice however if one side of the family is more well-off than the other or one is having financial problems, so tread lightly to avoid bruised egos.

Customized Contributions. If you're in doubt as to your parents' financial situation, ask if they want to contribute to a specific piece of the wedding. Your parents may offer to pay for the reception meal and your future in-laws might put in for the bar tab. It's okay to compartmentalize different aspects of the wedding and allow different parties to pay for separate things. Just remember, your parents might want a say about what you serve if they're footing the food bill.

And You Thought Talking About Sex Was Tough!

Talking about money is awkward and uncomfortable. Especially when you're discussing the big bucks that go into planning a wedding. If you're lucky, your parents will let you know right from the get-go how much they've stashed away for your big day. If you're not lucky and they stay silent despite the wedding ideas you share, you're going to have to take a deep breath and come out and ask them. When you do, it's important to broach the subject with tact, grace, and maybe a bit of ass kissing. Sit your parents down and have a frank discussion. Explain to them what you'd like your wedding to be like—and ask them whether they feel comfortable contributing financially. Traditionally, the bride's parents pay for the wedding, but in this day and age, it's perfectly acceptable to ask both sides of the family to contribute if you feel comfortable doing so.

If your folks say they want to help you out, ask them what they'd like to give. Their answer could vary. They might say half the total. They might give you a dollar amount. They might have to get back to you after they sell what they can on eBay. Whatever it is, get a number. Add that to whatever other money you have (or that is coming in) for your wedding spending. Then, take the total and subtract 10 percent—that's your budget. Be sure to take off that 10 percent because there are *always* unexpected costs that crop up and with quite a bit of extra padding, you won't be tempted to donate plasma or your fiancé's sperm in order to pay your wedding bills.

And you thought you'd never use math when you grew up!

Budget Breakdown

One of the hardest, yet most important, parts of a wedding budget is figuring out how much to spend on each piece of the wedding puzzle. So where do you start? So glad you asked.

TYPICAL BUDGET BREAKDOWN

- **Ceremony, 2 percent:** (site, marriage license, officiant, ceremony accessories, and rentals)
- **Reception, 45 percent:** (site, food, beverages, cake, rentals)
- **Attire and beauty, 10 percent:** (bride's gown and alterations, headpiece, veil, accessories, undergarments, hair, makeup, groom's tux or suit, groom's accessories)
- **Flowers, 8 percent:** (bride's and bridesmaids' bouquets, groom's and groomsmen's boutonnieres, flower girl's flowers, boutonnieres and corsages for VIPs, ceremony décor, reception centerpieces, and other reception décor)

- **Music, 8 percent:** (ceremony, cocktail hour, and reception musicians)
- **Photography and Videography, 12 percent:** (day fees, albums, prints, videos)
- **Transportation and Lodging, 3 percent:** (transportation for the wedding party, guest shuttle, parking attendants, wedding night accommodations for the bride and groom)
- **Stationery, 3 percent:** (save-the-dates, invitations, thank-you notes, postage, calligraphy, escort cards, table numbers, guest book, etc.)
- **Gifts and Favors, 3 percent:** (gifts for parents and wedding party, favors, welcome baskets for out-of-town guests)
- **Rings, 2 percent:** (wedding bands for the bride and groom)
- **Miscellaneous, 4 percent:** (all that other stuff that comes up along the way)

Ways to Keep Track so You'll Stay on Track

Now that you see where the money goes (um, hello reception), let me state that you don't have to use this breakdown as gospel since the amounts each engaged couple spends on each part of the wedding puzzle can differ greatly. For guidance, go back to that convo you had with your guy about the priorities of your wedding day and remember what the top three are. For instance, there's a big difference in costs between Champagne and Prosecco, a band and a DJ, and peonies and plastic flowers, so you can spend or save depending on your biggest desires.

The other tough part of a budget is sticking to it, so you must keep track as you go. This means implementing some sort of system. There are websites such as TheKnot .com and Brides.com with online budget tools that can help you out. There's also software specially designed to track wedding budgets. I personally like a good 'ol Excel spreadsheet. It's completely customizable, so you can create columns for whatever you want, adding in notes and even contact information for each vendor. Of course, if you haven't joined the rest of us in the modern era, you could use simple pen and paper. This most likely means that you're Amish and that your costs will no doubt be low anyway.

> "I never knew how anal my now-husband was until he created the 'super spreadsheet' to keep track of our budget. He even used pie charts so we could see what percentage we were spending on each type of item. I thought it was cute back then, but now that we're married, his budget spreadsheets drive me insane."
>
> —Jeanette

Whenever you make any kind of purchase or sign any kind of contract, keep the paperwork (including the receipt). Stay organized by storing everything in one place, whether it's a folder, giant envelope, or binder. I personally have found the sophisticated cardboard box system very helpful, so that you don't have to root through half your house to try to find the contract when you can't remember whether or not the florist is also bringing flowers to put on the cake.

Save: The Worst Four-Letter Word of All

Because even the best laid plans tend to go off track, you'll likely want to prepare for the unexpected and save, save, save all you can before the big day. I know we've all had to tighten our belts before, but now that you're trying to lose a few pounds to fit into a dress, you may be able to tighten that belt even further. Here are some ideas how:

- First, decide how much you need to save each month or each week to reach your savings goal.
- Start a savings account especially for wedding-related savings.
- Make sure you're putting that money aside. Either make an electronic transfer each month, or have part of your paycheck directly deposited into that account each payday.
- Find little ways to cut back in your everyday life. Paint your own nails. Pack your lunch and eat dinner at home. Clip coupons. You'll be amazed how small savings can add up!
- Check your bills. Are there any monthly expenses you can cut back on? Isn't giving up cable for a few months worth having a few luxuries at your wedding? You'll barely have time to watch TV anyhow.
- Ask for a raise. If you've been performing well and it's about time, why not? Just remember: no wedding planning while you're at work or you may find yourself wondering how you're going to pay for a

wedding while scraping by on unemployment benefits.

- Consider a short-term investment. There are three-, six-, nine-, and twelve-month CDs that you can purchase. After the designated time period, you're guaranteed to have made a certain percentage off them. An awesome way to get a little more bang for your buck, eh?

A WEDDING PLANNER: NOT JUST FOR J. LO

Anyone who knows about weddings or is a fan of J. Lo films knows there are wonderful people called wedding planners that have the potential to help take the "suck" out of planning your big day. That's because no matter how many decisions you love to make, there will always be ridiculously tough ones. And no matter how crafty you are, tying ribbons on 250 programs will quickly lose its appeal—especially after you've tied those ribbons on all the invitations and the favor boxes too. You will need help along the way. It will keep you sane and positive and keep wedding planning from taking over your whole life.

True, you can ask your friends and family to assist, but sometimes that can be more hell than help. That's where a wedding planner comes in. I know the idea of paying someone a hefty fee may seem extravagant, but wedding planners (hopefully!) know their nuptial stuff. They're creative, know who the good vendors are, and have loads of wedding experience that, unless you're Pamela Anderson, you most likely *don't* have. This is probably the first time you've had to pick out a wedding cake or figure out what time to tell your photographer to show up to an event.

Many people are hesitant to hire a wedding planner because it's another vendor to add to the list and thus another expenditure to add to the wedding budget. But women are great rationalizers (just look at how many shoes we have in our closets). One good rationalization is that a wedding planner can save you the man hours it takes to research videographers and tour venues that aren't remotely what you had in mind. Wedding planners already know good vendors and sites and can effectively edit choices down for you. They might be able to negotiate discounts and deals with certain vendors—especially the ones they have good relationships with—so there's a possibility you could make up for their fee along the way. There's also the cost of your sanity. I'm not saying you *need* a wedding planner, but you shouldn't immediately rule it out just because you think it's extraneous, or because you hated that J. Lo flick.

If one or more of these sound like you, you might want some hired help:

- You have a full-time and hectic job.
- You're getting married in less than eight months.
- Your future mother-in-law and/or mother is itching to take over the wedding planning.
- You don't like asking for help.
- You plan to have more than three vendors.
- You don't handle stress well.
- You'd like to lose weight, clear up your acne, and/or grow your fingernails before the wedding day.

- You'd like to avoid gaining weight, breaking out, and/or decimating your nails before the wedding day.
- You have no idea where to begin.
- You don't consider yourself a creative person.
- You don't consider yourself a detail-oriented person.
- You have trouble making decisions.
- You and your fiancé both have strong and differing opinions on how the wedding should go and you want to actually still be together by the time the big day arrives.

How to Find a Wedding Planner

If you think using a wedding planner is the way to go, how can you find one that's right for you? Good question. Here's a good answer: Always start with recommendations from someone whose wedding you admired. If you can't get a word of mouth recommendation, your next option is to hit the Yellow Pages or Google, or look at some online vendor databases. (TheKnot.com, Brides.com, WeddingWire.com, and local bridal magazines' websites are good places to start.) You might also try browsing the credentials of members of an organization such as the Association of Bridal Consultants (BridalAssn.com).

Once you have a few wedding planners in mind, check out their websites. When I wrote for regional bridal magazines, I found wedding planners' websites to be very revealing—if they're jumbled, disorganized, and outdated in design, what does that say about the wedding they'll plan? Also, many of the planners' sites will include photos from their previous events. If décor is an important element to you, check out the decorations they've done for past weddings. If it's a large, formal affair you're after, be sure the wedding planner has previous experience with similar events.

Once you have a few planners you'd like to meet, start interviewing them. Make sure you like their personality, their planning style, and of course the price for their services. Personality is vitally important. No matter how high profile or ultra-organized the wedding planner is, if the sound of her voice makes your skin crawl, by the time the wedding rolls around—and you'll have had 147 conversations with her—you might be ready to scratch your own eyes out. Weddings are complex, stressful occasions, punctuated by a rollercoaster of emotions. Choose someone who seems calming, on top of things, and just generally pleasant to be around.

Once you've decided you can get along, ask the wedding planner about her services and fees. Ask her about the kind of vendors she has relationships with—are they in your price range as well? Has she planned a wedding similar to the one you're envisioning before? How many weddings does she plan a year? What is her working style—will she meet with you often, chat over the phone, or e-mail? Exactly what services are included in her fees and what can be added on? What will be her duties on the actual wedding day?

It's an excellent idea to hire someone who's going to give you a lot of attention, who'll develop a vision and theme for your wedding day, and will handle the details of the planning with ease. A good wedding planner has quality vendors at her fingertips (and doesn't take kickbacks from them), and works well with them. She's planned plenty of weddings before and isn't overscheduled (stay away from hiring someone who's got another wedding planned that weekend). She can give you advice on etiquette, style choice, and logistics.

She should be able to create a timeline for the wedding day and be there on the day-of to accept deliveries, help set up equipment, and ensure everything runs on schedule.

Remember that some wedding planners offer a variety of different services. Some are paid a flat fee for helping out with everything necessary to plan the wedding. Others offer package deals with different amounts of services included in them. Sometimes the planning of other parties, such as the rehearsal dinner and next-day brunch, can be added to their packages. Some offer concierge-type services, where they can charge you for anything you need—like and envelope stuffing and favor assembling—on an hourly basis. And others can be hired just to create a schedule and show up on the wedding day to make sure everything runs smoothly.

When you've hired your wedding planner, make sure you go over the contract you have with her very carefully. Know what she's going to be planning and what your responsibilities are. For example, some wedding planners will help you choose your and your bridesmaids' gowns, but often you're on your own with these tasks. Know how many staffers she'll have helping out on your big day. Know what her backup plan is—what if she can't make the wedding due to unforeseen circumstances? Also, be aware of the payment plan. Most likely, you'll have to pay a deposit for her services, and the rest of the amount will be due on the big day.

Hiring a wedding planner can definitely help keep you sane. These party-savvy divas aren't miracle workers—there are still things that will be stressful along the way—but they usually have planned tons of weddings. And you haven't. Therefore, they can do the things that you don't know how to do, like find an awesome chef in your price range who knows how to make both seafood platters and taco bars so that you and your fiancé can both eat your favorite food at the reception (or at least *try* to eat because, after all the meeting and greeting you'll do, neither of you will eat a bite of food at your reception. More on that later.).

DON'T BE A SUPER BRIDE

What if you can't afford a wedding planner or you decide that you don't want one? That's cool, but if you don't have a wedding planner, you're still going to need some help. I understand why you don't want to send Aunt Suzy on your cake tasting or let your little brother pick out the guests' favors. That's the fun stuff that you don't want to miss. And let's face it, not everyone has as incredibly impeccable taste as you have. But you do want to delegate some of the other chores so you won't get so overwhelmed that you start crying in your shower every morning. For example, let your fiancé choose some tasks he'd like to do—honeymoon booking and transportation choices are popular for guys, but it can be anything. If he's creative, let him choose an invitation design instead. If your overbearing sister wants something to do, ask her to help you stuff the invitation envelopes on a rainy Saturday afternoon. Have a favor assembling party with a few of your closest girlfriends. If your mom is organized, have her make the confirmation calls. Take advantage of the talents and offerings of others so you're available for the really fun stuff like cake tasting. Even though many aspects of planning your wedding can suck, there is actually some fun to be had as well.

CHAPTER 2

Because Throwing Darts at a Map Won't Work for This

Location, location, location. This well coined phrase isn't just for real estate; it's crucial for wedding planning as well. Whether you've imagined an intimate afternoon affair at a restaurant or a nighttime soiree in a fancy hotel, your wedding location will solidify the feel of the whole event (plus eat up the majority of your wedding budget!). That's why there's enormous pressure to agree upon, and secure, the perfect location.

For a lot of couples, the first step in the journey is deciding on the city or town where the wedding will take place. If you both have friends and family in the same location, this is easy. But if your fiancé grew up in one part of the world, and you're from another, deciding on a location can be worse than having your period on your honeymoon (more on that good stuff in Chapter 8). Agreeing on a location is a common dilemma since many of us strive to move far away from our parents after high school (only to move closer once our first kid is born to capitalize on all the free babysitting). If you're both from different towns and can't agree on one location, you can have a ceremony in both places, pick just one and piss half the people off, or have it in an entirely neutral location and piss *everyone* off.

The location of the event can influence the time of year during which you decide your wedding take should place. If you've always dreamed of an outdoor wedding and live in Southern California, chances are you're good to go. But if your wedding will take place during a Minnesota winter, you can only pray Vera Wang comes out with a bridal parka and silken snow pants.

Costs are also a big consideration and can vary greatly depending on the locale. A fancy hotel wedding in a big city will cost way more than one in a small town where the term "fancy" is used to refer to the motel that offers free ice. My groom and I spent a third of what we would have spent in New York by having our do-over reception in my hometown outside Pittsburgh. However, keep in mind that having the festivities far from where you reside can add to the overall expense since you might have to plan trips to tour locations and interview vendors. It's also more of a pain in the butt since you'll have to travel with your wedding dress, your guy's tux, and maybe even wedding gear like favors, decorations, and so on. I even hauled a bridesmaid on the seven-hour drive with me.

BALLROOM BLITZ

No doubt the most popular venue for weddings is a ballroom setting. Sure, they're cookie cutter, have hideous carpeting, and remind everyone of the place where the tenth grade Sadie Hawkins dance was held. But they're certainly the easiest because they have everything you need at their disposal: tables, chairs, linens, fully equipped kitchens, moveable dance floors, and tons of experienced staff. They're basically your one-stop shop of wedding venues. Not only are they all-inclusive, but they're also very forgiving for your wedding. If it's snowing outside, who cares? You can still wear a strapless gown. If you want to party long into the night, no worries. There's plenty of light and no mosquitoes in sight.

Its blah 1986-style lighting fixtures aside, a ballroom setting is a good place to hold both the ceremony *and* the reception because rooms are easily manipulated. Guests can watch you walk down the aisle and say "I do" underneath a lovely chuppah and then go out on a patio for a few cocktails. When they reenter the room, it's magically transformed into a dining room with tables for dinner. It's like watching a Broadway performance!

Another bonus? Ballrooms are often in or near hotels, making it extra easy for you to plan since you won't have to arrange shuttle busses or other transportation to and from hotels. It's also extra easy for the out-of-town guests who can be close to the action, get piss drunk at the wedding, and find their way safely to bed without having to hunt down a designated driver.

Since ballroom management is so in tune with the wedding industry, most of them can plan the event with one chocolate-fountain-fondue-covered hand tied around their back. Usually, there's an in-house event planner who can work with you on all the details. At the very least, the planner will have a list of recommended vendors who they often work with that you can choose from. But most of them will actually offer complete packages that include dinner, bar, cake, waitstaff, center-pieces, and so on. Getting a package deal often is cheaper than having to pay for everything a la carte. Also, having your cake baker, caterer, florist, and bartenders already picked out saves you a lot of time, energy, and stress (just think how much your complexion will thank you). Just be sure to check out the vendors' work first so you won't be locked into a fried Twinkie wedding cake because it's the only thing the resident "baker" knows how to make—unless, of course, you've always dreamed of you and your new husband cutting into a ridiculous mound of preservative-filled snack cakes.

Sure, the package thing can be limiting, but the good news is, if you don't like the package your ballroom offers, you can negotiate some changes. Ask how much less they'll charge if you don't use the in-house baker (although, seriously, a fried Twinkie cake sounds pretty damn good to me). Remember to look over what's included in the package carefully. If there are any extras you don't want or that are overpriced, ask if they can be removed or renegotiated and if you can be charged slightly less. Nothing should be set in stone when it comes to packages and haggling is almost always allowed.

Also, look over your contract to see what's *not* there. Your ballroom might not offer some things you *do* want, like an upgrade to silk linens, special lighting, or an ice sculpture carved in the image of you and your groom. Make sure you're allowed to bring in outside vendors to provide those extras, and also make sure that the site won't charge you additional fees to use those outside services. Ideas for your ballroom wedding:

Wear a silk-satin ball gown with elaborate beading paired with a sparkly tiara.

Decorate with luxurious layered fabrics in rich jewel tones and oodles of lush roses.

Eat crowd pleasers like petite filet and roasted chicken.

Get sweet with a towering confection covered in a cascade of flower petals. A traditional bride and groom cake topper is a classic touch.

Get away in a chic limousine.

WATER LOGGED

Ah, a waterfront wedding. Whether it's beachside, lakeside, riverside, or creekside, nothing beats the relaxed nature of nuptials better than . . . well, nature. Just picture it: Walking barefoot down the sandy aisle to exchange your "I do"s. Cocktails on the edge of a dock or on a gorgeous boat. A casual dinner overlooking a stunning sunset. Waterfront weddings have been the staples of every bridal magazine published and the setting for a cheese-tastic Katherine Heigl movie. But it can also be a frustratingly unpredictable locale. Coastal fog and sudden cold fronts can be quite uncomfortable, and do I have to point out the unforgivable things humidity can do to hair and makeup? Just as with drinking and text messaging, mixing water and weddings can have a horrible outcome.

But if you're a go-with-the-flow kind of bride who's marrying a go-with-the-flow kind of guy (or one that knows the power of the phrase "whatever you want, dear"), then start planning your waterfront wedding. There are a number of ways you can do it:

- Choose a hotel or resort that's on the water and use its staff to help you plan the event.
- Find a public beach that gives out permits for holding events and probe the local government to find out its rules and regulations.

- Book a seaside restaurant, boat club, or event space.
- Beg or bribe a friend or relative who has a waterfront home to host your big day.

"The fantasy was a 'calm and peaceful' spring beach wedding. The reality was a fan stuck between my boobs while I straddled an AC vent to cool off as my bridesmaids fed me tequila shots from the yet unopened bar in an effort to make it all go away."

—Melissa

Just a few words of wisdom: Any outdoor wedding should always have a Plan B in case of bad weather. This means you actually need to plan two weddings, but an ounce of prevention (as well as waterproof mascara) is worth a pound of cure.

Ideas for your beach wedding:

Wear a flowing slip dress, sandals or nothing on your feet, and skip the veil.

Decorate with pretty shells, elegant tin pails, and exotic white orchids.

Eat chilled seafood from a massive raw bar.

Get sweet with coconut cake with pineapple filling, topped with two happy clams (made of sugar) to represent you and your guy.

Get away in a dune buggy—or kayak!

GOIN' TO THE CHAPEL

Weddings that take place in houses of worship are rich with longstanding traditions and the wonderful, spiritual sentiments that religion can offer. They're also usually really cheap. Some houses of worship are old fashioned, with high ceilings, intricate statues, and stained glass windows, while others are more contemporary and look like cutting-edge theaters equipped with sophisticated sound systems—and many fall somewhere in between. If you're already a member of a church, temple, synagogue, or other congregation, then it's safe to say that's where you'll choose to get married if you want to go the religious route. But if you're not—or your wedding will be in another town—then you'll have to seek out an alternate venue.

Sure, you can choose a place based on its looks, but you also want to find one that will offer you what you want from your ceremony. Make sure you vibe with the clergy and that you like the service and music they offer. Some houses of worship may actually require that you *become* a member in order to get married there, which could mean extra costs, and maybe extra guilt when you sleep through that week's service—but in general, this might still be a very affordable option. You may only be asked to make a small donation to the church and then be left to deal with that lifelong guilt (and possible eternal damnation, too).

Be aware that weddings in religious settings can range from a little bit restrictive to downright stodgy. Often, you must reserve your date an entire year in advance, rendering a shotgun wedding out of the question. You might not be able to write your own vows or choose untraditional music for your ceremony, so if you're dying to go dancin' down the aisle a la that YouTube sensation, ask your officiant what parts of the ceremony are malleable. Even the strictest religions may allow a little leeway. For example, maybe you have to say the traditional Catholic vows, but you can add some of your own words during another part of the ceremony. Other rules might not be so flexible. Some might not allow your photographer to use a flash or stand in certain spots while capturing the event. Others may have rules that restrict alcohol. I was a brides-maid for a wedding in a church that didn't allow booze on the premises so the bride got gypped out of that all-important, nerve reducing, pre-ceremony champagne toast in the bride's room. Now *that's* a sin!

> **"My fiancé and I both wanted to have the traditional long Catholic ceremony for our wedding. We knew some people would moan and complain, but what we didn't expect is for some of them to bring their iPods along to keep themselves entertained."**
>
> **—Sarah**

The downside of having your ceremony in a house of wor-ship is that you'll probably have to have your reception at an entirely different location (although the church hall or base-ment wedding *does* still exist in some communities). This means schlepping the guests to another venue. Talk about wedding interruptus! There's a certain emotional flow to a wedding that can be destroyed due to the stress of rush hour traffic or lost guests. Plus, there can be a significant amount of time after the church wedding ends and before you're allowed into your reception, and what else is there for guests to do but hit happy hour and get loaded? However, with some good planning and a few answered prayers, a church wedding can be a wonderful way to start your life together.

I LIKE MY POTATOES—AND MY WEDDINGS— HOME-STYLE, THANK YOU

If you really want a homey feel to your wedding, you should consider having your wedding at home. Duh. Whether it's your place, your parents', or some distant relative's to-die-for house, an at-home wedding is personal and can have either the feel of an intimate cocktail party or a breezy summer picnic. It's all in how you plan it.

The biggest mistake people make that turns around to bite them in the behind is thinking that at-home weddings will save them money. These are the people who never saw the Steve Martin classic, *Father of the Bride*. While there is no rental site fee, there are plenty of other incidentals that can add up fast such as tables, chairs, linens, tents, decorations, heat lamps, dishes, utensils, and stemware.

The good news is it's easy to make the space feel like your own, because, obviously, it is. Choose a special spot for the ceremony like underneath the oak tree that you climbed as a kid, in front of the fireplace where you shared great family moments, or outside in the gazebo where you and your fiancé snuck in a quickie during the "meet my parents" weekend. Bay windows, balconies, and scenic views also make excellent backdrops. You can even mix it up a bit: have cocktails in the house or on a pretty spot on the lawn—then guests can walk to a backyard tent for dinner and dancing.

Before you commit to an at-home wedding, realize it's a lot more labor intensive than a wedding in a hotel or other venue. There's a lot of prep work and cleanup that you'll either have to do yourself or hire staff to take care of. Make sure you truly have the facilities to make this happen. Most people don't have a gourmet kitchen fit for a catering staff to prepare dinner, so outside kitchen items (grills, cooktops, etc.) will probably need to be brought in and the menu may have to be adjusted. You may not have enough parking spaces for everyone. If not, is there a nearby parking lot where valets can bring the cars? How about bathrooms? Nothing says sucky wedding more than forcing your guests to "hold it" standing in a long bathroom line. Can you rent some portable bathrooms? I know it sounds like an oxymoron, like jumbo shrimp or comfortable heels, but fancy portable bathrooms do exist (check the resource section in the back for details).

   Ideas for your at-home wedding:

   Wear your mom's gown—or a pretty, lacy number that could pass as a family heirloom.

   Decorate with crystals hung from tree branches, family photos of the both of you on the mantel, and home-grown flowers.

   Eat entrees inspired by classic family recipes. Yes, your caterer may be able to recreate your fiancé's grandma's ravioli recipe, or your mom's famous empanadas.

   Get sweet with home-style frosted cupcakes decorated with butter cream and sugar tulips.

   Get away in Uncle Fred's vintage convertible Mustang.

TABLE FOR TWO . . . HUNDRED

If you and your fiancé are big foodies, or you're sentimental and want to have your wedding where you had your first date or where he proposed, a restaurant wedding is just the thing. The setting is smaller and more intimate and the food is almost always better than at banquet halls or catered events where the makeshift kitchens consist of what appears to be Bunsen burners and Easy Bake Ovens.

Restaurants play host to tons of parties, so why not a wedding too? Not only will it make your life easier to find one that's held a wedding before, but they might even have menus and packages already set up. They may have private rooms and a dance floor. Valet parking shouldn't be a problem, and there will be enough bathroom stalls to accommodate your guests. Space may be tight at restaurants, so the size of your guest list might be limited, but that could be a good thing for both your wallet and the overall feel of your event.

"We got married at a restaurant that served my husband's favorite spicy chicken. It was six years ago, and to this day my husband is still pissed at me that I made him go chat with guests at our wedding before he was done eating."

—Sarah

If you're marrying at a restaurant, be sure to ask lots of questions about restrictions and fees. For example, the management might charge you a corkage fee or cake-cutting fee for the extra staff it takes to pour champagne and slice and serve wedding cake. Your bar bill might also skyrocket, since restaurants tend to mark up the price of booze and often don't allow you to bring in your own bottles. Being aware of these extra expenses up front will prevent you from

having to dine on a steady stream of Ramen noodles and
Rice-a-Roni the first year of your marriage just to pay off
your Top Chef–worthy wedding.

Ideas for your restaurant wedding:

Wear a silk tank-style cocktail dress. (Strapless might
keep slipping down while you're sitting for an extended,
many-course dining experience.)

Decorate with bountiful centerpieces made with food.
Citrus fruits, apples, artichokes, and other edible stuff are
pretty compliments to flowers.

Eat your chef's specialty. Let your pro do what he or she
does best—that's why you chose this restaurant, right?

Get sweet with gourmet plated desserts whipped up by
the in-house pastry chef. Guests can choose between something fruity, like a raspberry tart, and something chocolately,
like a decadent mousse.

Get away in your own car, polished especially for the
event. (You can even have someone do the tin can thing if
you want.)

A LOFTY IDEA

If you find more traditional venues to be a bore, you can
customize your own wedding by looking for a location
that's a blank slate, such as a loft or a hall. Loft spaces are
essentially big, empty rooms that you can design to suit
your own style and needs. You could have a huge dance
floor, or long, family-style tables for dinner, or even pony
rides and bouncies if that's your cup of tea.

If you don't live in an urban area with lofts readily available, rent out the fire hall or the church hall. Okay, so they're

not always the most attractive options, but they're usually fantastically affordable. That's where your creativity, or that of your wedding planner, will come in. Just keep in mind that you'll have to bring in most everything you'll need. Sure, if you're looking for a casual, kitschy-style event, a fire hall's fold-up tables and plastic drinking glasses may work just fine, but some brides don't think a disposable champagne flute with a pop off bottom exactly screams "wedding."

Remember that blank or underdressed settings like lofts or halls may need tons of decorations to make them look as beautiful and personalized as you want your wedding to be. You'll probably want to hang decorations from the ceilings, string twinkle lights, and use lots of lush fabrics and flowers. The costs for renting or purchasing this stuff can really add up. I would strongly suggest hiring a wedding planner if you want to create a wedding from a blank canvas like this. He or she will probably have tons of ideas for making the space lovely and memorable. True, you could just do it yourself, but as someone who often writes about how to "do it yourself," but then ends up *screwing* it up myself, I would be very intimidated to pull off a wedding in a place like this.

Ideas for your blank slate wedding:

Wear a gown that looks like it walked off this season's runway. Play up the urban vibe.

Decorate by mixing metals with clear acrylic. Choose sleek, cylindrical vases with boldly colored blooms.

Eat heavy hors d'oeuvres. Make sure guests know it will be cocktails and munchies only—no dinner.

Get sweet with bite-sized petit fours, decorated with modern shapes. Have a trendy cake made with your city's skyline drawn around each tier.

Get away by hailing a taxi.

NACHO ORDINARY VENUES

The previously mentioned venues are the most popular wedding location options, but really, the sky's the limit. You don't have to be traditional or customary here. Think of places that you and your fiancé love—then call their manager and ask if they do weddings. The more unique and "you" your wedding is, the more personalized and memorable the day will be.

How 'bout a wedding at a country club? Often you need to be a member of the club—or a relative does—in order to book it. But if you've got it, flaunt it! A country club is perfect for that quaint-yet-elegant prepster feel. Often, there's gorgeous landscaping and/or golf greens that make for fantastic photo ops. At the end of the night, drive off in a golf cart with a sign that says "just married."

Museums and art galleries have got quite a bit of wow factor, too. Imagine guests dining beside the bones of a massive brontosaurus or nibbling hors d'oeuvres while perusing the work of local modern artists. Just be sure that you know about every restriction going in. For example, you might not be able to serve red wine or have any food whatsoever in certain parts of the venue so that the exhibits and artwork won't get damaged. However, guests may soon forget those rules while they're gazing at the homoerectus recreation. Other similarly captivating options include planetariums, zoos, science centers, and aquariums.

You can also rent out a historic home or other property for your wedding day. The type of home it is will greatly influence the style of wedding that takes place there. For example, it could be a charming country house that you've always fantasized about owning, and you'll actually own it

. . . for a day anyway. Or it could be a luxurious mansion or castle straight out of a Harlequin romance novel. A wedding there would be fit for royalty and will make you and your groom feel like king and queen for a day. Then there's the option of a quaint farm wedding. You can have an upscale pig roast, dine by candlelight in a barn, and cap off the night by roasting marshmallows over a bonfire with your guests.

"While my mom and I were wedding dress shopping, we were talking to another bride about our weddings. It turned out they were scheduled on the same place on the same day—like something out of *Bride Wars!* My mom and I raced over to the country club who admitted they messed up and had to find out whose deposit check had cleared first. Luckily, it was mine. Crazy!"

—Karen

And what about a wedding at a winery? Stunning vineyards, excellent food, upscale service . . . and of course, there's all that vino! What could be finer? Bring home a case of their new vintage and every year on your anniversary, open up a bottle and look at your wedding album in front of a fire. C'mon! What's more romantic than that?

A FOREIGN AFFAIR

Some time during the last decade or so, destination weddings became a hot item. This is where a couple will hightail

it to Tahiti or Hawaii or Paris or Rio or some other romantic, exotic, nostalgic, or otherwise meaningful locale to get
hitched. To top off the logistical challenge, they bring along
their bridesmaids, parents, siblings, and BFFs. That's a whole
lotta crazy waiting to happen. But if you're set on a foreign
affair, here are some strategies for getting through it.

First, choose a destination with minimal hassle. Hawaii
and Puerto Rico are good choices because they're part of the
United States and fairly routine places for Americans to get
a marriage license and make it legal (if you're not American, then it's a whole other banana). It's more complicated
to legally get hitched abroad in popular places like France
and Mexico—you might have to marry in the native language, whether you speak it or not, and you might need
special permission from local lawmakers or just be required
to complete a mountain of paperwork. So if you're choosing
one of those destinations, might I suggest heading to your
local city hall to make it legal, and then having an unofficial
wedding ceremony in the foreign country of your choice?
Sounds like it's cheating I know, but a lot of couples do it
and don't tell anyone, which makes it even hotter. Remember on *The Office* when Pam and Jim snuck off and had the
Maid of the Mist captain marry them—aren't they adorable?
I'm not saying you shouldn't marry abroad: just be sure you
do the appropriate research on your particular destination
and fill out all necessary paperwork beforehand to be sure
you return home actually *married*, seeing how that is most
likely your goal.

Choosing a destination where your native tongue is spo-
ken will also be a tremendous help. If not, you'll need a
way to communicate with wedding vendors besides hand
gestures and talking really loudly. These days, many brides

wanting to plan a destination wedding will chose a venue they've been to before, such as a resort where they've vacationed. If not, they'll need to take a trip to the destination and tour a few locales. Or, if you can't make the trip, you can hire a wedding planner who's familiar with the area to do the dirty work. Not only can she be your stand-in (as long as you completely trust her) for choosing a venue, she can help you with things that don't fall under the site manager's job description, such as arranging hotel transportation, planning a rehearsal dinner, and finding local vendors like an officiant, a cake baker, and musicians. Someone who is based there—or has planned plenty of weddings there before—is ideal. Of course, this isn't necessary, but it can help you breathe easier. When choosing your final location, don't just rely on websites. Between Photoshop, good lighting, and fake reviews, websites can make their ramshackle hotel appear to be a five-star location.

If you don't have the time or money to visit the country first, play it safe and choose a hotel brand that you know, such as Hilton or Ritz-Carlton, or any chain you know you like. Just be cautious of some mass market chain hotels that crank out weddings similar to the way Hostess cranks out Ding-Dongs. In order to save money, these look-a-like weddings can be quite impersonal and a little bit cheesy.

The good thing about planning at a resort that's experienced with weddings is that they often have easy-to-choose-from packages and site managers who are comfortable with helping couples plan everything that happens at the resort via phone and e-mail. I suggest you get yourself a good international calling plan, or sign up with Skype, because there will be a whole lot of long distance calls going on. Remember that you can go beyond the typical touristy resort. There are some really unique venues in other lands as well, and their staff can work with you to plan your destination wedding. Maybe it's a historical landmark, the top of a mountain in a national park, or even the deck of a cruise ship where you can be queen of the world! Or at least, queen for a day.

Ideally, you'll want to factor into your budget at least one trip to the destination during the planning period. This is a good time to meet with vendors and check out their work. Ask your site if you can peek in on a bash that's being held there while you're in town. Check out the flowers the florist works with—do they look fresh and lovely? I was once in Aruba and visited a flower shop that only had carnations and cacti. Do you really want carnations and cacti for your wedding? Does the cake baker create gorgeous confections or something that looks like it belongs on the day-old sales rack at your local supermarket? Once you hire your destination wedding vendors, it's important to get everything in writing (as with *every* wedding vendor) and read over all contracts carefully (this is where speaking the language comes in handy). Then, be sure to arrive at the destination a few days before your wedding day so you can visit vendors, review the plans, and go over any last minute details. The few extra days will also allow you to get used to the time change so you won't need to reschedule your evening wedding for three in the afternoon so you can stay awake for it.

Make all the same travel arrangements you would if you were planning a regular old vacation to your destination. Be sure you've updated your passports and visas, and met any other travel requirements well in advance of the wedding day—and that everyone in your wedding party does as well. You'll also want to check out the recommended vaccinations for your destination and make an appointment to get all your shots. It would be good to prevent a sudden onset of malaria or some other exotic disease, don't you think?

Since you'll probably be flying to your destination, it's important to call your airline beforehand and check regulations for carry-ons and checked packages. For example, if you're planning on bringing along gifts or favors, they'll need to be packed unwrapped because of security rules. You will probably be able to carry on your gown, but you might have to fight other passengers for dibs on using the tiny onboard closet to hang it in.

Now for your guests. No, you're not required to pay for guests' airfare or hotel, but don't expect everyone to be able to attend. People will have to take vacation days and pay big bucks to make the trip, so be appreciative, dammit! Don't take their attendance for granted or act like a diva because you didn't receive as many place settings for gifts as you wanted. As for the people who do attend, consider planning events for them; maybe a tour of a local brewery or a pool party rehearsal dinner. However, also let them have time on their own because while your wedding does mean a lot to them, it very well might be the only trip they get to take this whole year.

Listen, once you've gotten this whole location thing out of the way, you'll be able to breathe a whole lot easier. It's like getting Freshman Comp, Phys Ed, and your foreign language requirement done during your first semester of college. After that, you've got more direction and you can concentrate on the courses (a.k.a. wedding details) that, to you, are more fun. Oh yeah, and the beer too. Don't forget the beer.

CHAPTER 3

Checking Your List Twice Without the Help of Santa or Other Magical Beings

Location and guest list size go hand-in-hand. Chances are you had at least a general idea of how many people you wanted to invite before you chose a venue, since you most likely wanted one large enough to fit all your guests, but now that you've booked the venue, it's time to fine-tune exactly who's on the list. Be warned, creating that all important guest list is a task that sparks more controversy than the swine flu vaccine shortage and causes epic battles among engaged couples and their families.

A guest list isn't written in stone, and, until you actually mail out the invitations, can evolve more than Brad Pitt's face did in *Benjamin Button*. Perhaps, against all odds, you were able to book that elusive Grand Ballroom and can now expand your list, or you fell in love with the idea of having your wedding at the intimate restaurant where he proposed, despite an endless list of friends and family.

All guest lists should start by compiling a list of "must invites":

- Start with your nearest and dearest. Your parents, grandparents and siblings. Your fiancé's parents, grandparents, and siblings. Your BFFs. Ask yourselves who you couldn't possibly get married without.
- If you're ready for more, branch out into the close friends category and extended family like aunts, uncles, and first cousins.
- Find a good place to draw the line. The "must invite list" should have a distinct delineation. For example aunts and uncles but not great aunts and uncles. College friends who live in your town and that you see often, but not ones you haven't talked to in a year.
- At this point, you have the minimum number of guests to invite. But, if you and your fiancé have room to keep going, write down more names in order of the most important to the least. When you hit the max number of people who can fit in your reception hall or who you can afford to have at your reception (it's almost always a per person price), you've got your list.

Does that sound way too easy? Well it can be—and will be if you have endless funds and it's clear cut who the most "important" people are in your life. But most often it's not, and this is where the trouble lies. I mean, my dad has eight brothers and sisters, and I have approximately *twenty-five* first cousins—just on that side of the family alone. That's almost fifty people right there. So if your family's Irish Catholic too, and you've got fifty people on one side, while your fiancé has exactly one aunt who never married or had kids, should he invite forty-nine not-so-close people so you guys are even-steven? What if you have a dozen relatives under the age of ten that you rarely see, and he has only one whom he's really close to? Do you invite all the rugrats or can you make an exception and just allow his? What if he has step-parents and half siblings and you're an only child and an orphan to boot? Can you now have license to invite your co-workers? I've learned many things about wedding planning, but I cannot begin to answer these particular questions for you. The best thing you can do is feel out your own situation and find ways to work through the issues that arise. If you and your fiancé or your family are clashing about the guest list—and you're bound to—there are several ways to help resolve your arguments:

- **Divide the list equally.** Maybe from the beginning, you and your fiancé get to choose a third of the guest list, your parents choose a third, and your in-laws choose a third. Of course, this may mean your dad's buddy from high school whom you've never met comes to your wedding, but many people find that division fair in theory. (Although, if you think about it, it's your wedding. Maybe you and your fiancé should have half and the parents should split the other half. This kind of thing really depends on you all and, often, who's paying. See below.)
- **Let the money talk.** If your parents are paying, you might have to suck it up and let them have their way. When those people you don't know walk through the receiving line, just smile, hug, thank them for coming,

and then thank God you didn't have to pay for their chicken florentine, or anyone else's for that matter.

- **Compare apples to apples.** You could argue that a first cousin is a first cousin, no matter what. Just because your fiancé has twenty-five and you have one doesn't mean that you should get to invite your second cousins.
- **Respect close bonds.** If it's immediate family only, but your guy has a godfather that's been like a second father to him, he should be able to invite him. There are always exceptions to rules.

Yeah, I know that I just contradicted myself in those points, but that's because the guest list is a very personal decision, and you need to find the best way to make these decisions for you, personally. I know it's tempting to invite everyone you've ever met and will ever see again to your wedding, but, unless you want to have your wedding in an open field and serve everyone bread and butter sandwiches, you have to draw the line. And speaking of bread and butter sandwiches . . .

FOLLOW THE MONEY

Not only is the guest list linked to the location, it's linked to the budget as well. In the ideal world of guest list writing, you have a budget, come up with an estimated number of guests, choose a location and, based on the fees associated with the venue, refine your guest list accordingly. However, things may not be so ideal. Maybe you have a very limited budget, but need to invite 300 of your nearest and dearest.

In that case you can forget about that Plaza wedding of your dreams and grill hot dogs and hamburgers in your backyard. It all goes back to the priorities that you and your fiancé have established.

Remember as you're considering your budget, that approximately 80 percent of the total invitees actually attend the wedding. I remember scoffing at this number when I was planning my own bash—I mean, that must be for your average wedding, but surely more people would attend *ours!* But in the end, it turned out that exactly 80 percent of our guests RSVP'd "yes." This isn't to say you should count on an 80 percent turnout. In fact, it's crucial that you be able to afford the wedding if everyone shows up, no matter what.

If you can't afford (or don't want) to invite all your friends, family, co-workers, their dates, and their small children, how do you draw the line? And, how do you and your fiancé agree on where to draw the line? As you can see, refining your guest list is like putting together a puzzle, a very political puzzle that can hurt a lot of feelings, break up friendships, and cause awkward silences at family gatherings for years to come. Again, I can't make these decisions for you, but I can provide some general guidelines that can make deciding easier. Or at least give you someone to blame when your third cousin twice removed is pissed at you for not including him. Here's some advice:

Couples. Naturally, married couples should always be invited together. Many people also think if a couple is engaged or living together, they should both be invited. Not everyone should expect to bring their "boyfriend" or "girlfriend," but if you know it's serious and/or they've been together for six months or more, consider inviting them, too. Also, avoid writing "and guest" on the invitation if at all possible. Always try to find out the name of the significant other before you send the invite.

Plus ones. Single guests never need to be invited with a guest but it's a nice thing to do if you have the space and the budget. Only do this if you can offer the option to all the single adults. Plus ones can get tricky, but if you're consistent, it will limit any hurt feelings.

Kids. Make a decision to invite kids or not invite them. If you're not inviting kids, you can always make exceptions for very close relatives, like your niece and nephew, especially if they're the ring bearer and flower girl. Also, in the case of teenagers, perhaps you can designate a cut off age, such as inviting those over sixteen.

Friends. It's tempting to want to invite all the pals you've ever made, but chances are you'll have to draw the line somewhere. I recommend clearly thinking about who will be there to celebrate your silver anniversary with you someday.

Co-workers. No, you don't have to invite your boss, but you might think you'll get in good with her if you do. If that's the case, it's okay. It's also okay to just invite the people from work who you see *outside* of work and not feel like you have to invite the whole department.

Your parents' and in-laws' friends. Again, if they're paying and they insist on inviting their friends, you might not have much choice. However, if that bumps some of *your* peeps off the list, maybe you should make a very nice plea to your parents to make some changes.

It may feel cruel to just slash someone off the list faster than you can say, "Pass the Sharpie," but most couples do have to cut people from their list. It's pretty much the easiest way to spend less on your wedding, so don't be shy. It sucks to have to explain to people that they're not invited or that they can't bring their adorable yet colicky Baby Jane, but you gotta do what you gotta do.

Again, go across the boards to keep things fair. Find groups to completely cut. Dates, kids, co-workers, and these other groups just mentioned are all fair game. Don't feel like you have to apologize to people who aren't invited. If they mention something to you, casually tell them that there are no kids allowed or that only engaged couples can bring dates, or even that you're limited to having a really small wedding. It's rare for people to go out of their way to confront you about not having to buy you a wedding gift or sit through a wedding mass, but it's been known to happen.

WHEN BEING ANAL-RETENTIVE WOULD REALLY COME IN HANDY

Okay, so you've got a bunch of names. Now you've got to come up with their accurate spelling, correct mailing addresses, the spelling of their spouses' and dates' names, and details like whether they go by Ms. or Mrs. Not such an easy task. Here's how to make it just a little bit easier:

Use a program like Excel where you can easily create columns for names street address, city, state, and zip code and fill in the details for each person. Later on, it's easy to merge this type of database with a Word document for addressing envelopes for invitations, thank-you notes, or even next year's holiday cards. (In fact, if you already have a database for holiday addresses, you're way ahead of where the rest of us were when we started compiling our guest lists. Yay for you.)

Ask questions. Don't just assume you know everything about everybody. Go to Mom and make sure Aunt Suzie isn't actually Aunt Suzy. Oh yeah, and ask whether her husband is Lewis or Louis.

Make others responsible. If your dad insisted that you invite his boss, put him in charge of getting the boss man's address and the name of his wife.

Check etiquette. There are lots of weird rules for addressing envelopes when it comes to different marital situations and relationships. Did you know if a woman is a Dr., her name goes *before* her husband's on the envelope? Some divorced women go by Ms. and others go by Mrs. Oh, and a married woman who has not changed her last name is *not* Mrs. plus her maiden name! I wish I could go over it all but these rules make up a whole book in and of themselves! Refer to *Emily Post's Etiquette* or *Emily Post's Wedding Etiquette* to find out how to deal with sticky guest list situations.

Update it all. If you've already got a list of names and addresses, remember that people move frequently. Go over each and every address and ask someone who'd know whether this is the most recent info for each guest. You don't want your beautiful invitation envelopes to come back to your mailbox, stamped undeliverable.

Have a proofreader—or two or three. Go over the list yourself to double-check the details. Then have your mom, your fiancé, or your mother-in-law (maybe even all three) double check things. You won't be totally screwing up if you spell a couple names wrong, but the fewer mistakes the better—both to avoid those returned invites and to avoid offending your cousin when you spell her name wrong on every Hanukah card you send her the rest of your life.

Work the inner envelope. If you've chosen one of those fancy invitations with an inner and outer envelope, you *are* supposed to write on the inner. Some people don't know that. You can write what you call the invitees ("Nana and Pap Pap") or you can use their formal titles ("Mr. and Mrs. Jorge Gonzales"). Be sure to put exactly who's invited here, since you don't want these peeps to think that they can bring along their two-year-old if kids aren't invited. Remember to try to find out any boyfriend/girlfriend/date's name before you send out the invite, unless of course, they don't know yet who they're taking.

Know that if you rush through the guest list—and the spelling of guests' names and addresses—it can show, making your invites feel a little less formal when they show up in people's mailboxes with misspellings and marks from the post office. So take a little extra time with it, and you won't get shunned at next year's family Easter egg hunt.

CHAPTER 4

It's Only A Dress—So Why Am I Spending Two Grand on It?

The cynic in me thinks it's sinful to spend thousands of dollars on a dress that you'll only wear once, but the romantic in me drools over duchesse satin and embroidered details. What woman wouldn't want to wear a one-of-a-kind gown that flatters every inch of her body, made of creamy white fabric so luxurious it creates a glow worthy of a princess? Sometimes I wish Gap Body would create a line of wedding sweat pants so I could feel like a bride while I'm vacuuming my apartment!

Yes, no woman can resist wearing a gown that should be hung in a museum. Sure, it will cost a few months' rent and is so delicate that you'll have to handle it more carefully than nitroglycerin. Also, once your wedding is over it will need to be packed by professionals and stored neatly in the bowels of your closet, never to be seen again. But, hell, it's worth it!

Enjoy this fantasy of that dress while you can. Savor the image of yourself gliding down a long staircase to your awaiting groom while all the ex-boyfriends who broke your heart and playground bullies who called you "four eyes" watch with gaping jaws. Now snap out of it because wedding dresses aren't all fairy tales and flattery. There's a lot involved in buying these few yards of fabric: a lot of dressing and undressing; a lot of squeezing and unsqueezing; a lot of opinions that might not vibe with yours. And, of course, a butt-load of money.

There's a hell of a lot of pressure to find *the* perfect dress. It's sure to be the most expensive outfit you'll ever own (unless you plan to clothe yourself in a Mercedes). It's the dress that will be judged by all your friends, family, and of course fiancé, and it's the dress that you'll be wearing in the photographs that will displayed on the wall above your fireplace for decades to come. Now that's quite a lot of pressure for one outfit.

HOW TO AVOID TAKING "SHOP 'TIL YOU DROP" LITERALLY

If you're lucky, you have an idea of where you want to buy your wedding dress. It's a store that you've stood outside, gazing longingly at the gowns in the window for years, or that adorable place where you bought your prom dress that carries amazing bridal gowns as well. If you're not that lucky and have no idea where to shop, ask a few friends, particularly the ones whose gowns you admired. Here's a secret: while it's important to choose somewhere that has a great selection in your price range, it's also crucial that it has good customer service. My friend ordered an amazing dress at a small boutique that didn't specialize in wedding dresses, and it ended up arriving too late to be properly altered. That's not a shop I'd recommend no matter how gorgeous the dress was.

There are several types of bridal stores to choose from. First, there's the independent bridal salon, like a mom and pop shop (but a more upscale mom and pop than the kind that live in a rundown trailer and floss with strands of their own hair). Expect to find a friendly staff there who'll give you lots of attention and help.

The selections at independent salons will vary. Some salons will carry a limited number of designers' and manu-facturers' gowns in a specific price range. Usually the price range will reflect what the local clientele tends to pur-chase most. Others will have a very large selection, in low, medium, and high budget options. I personally love the idea of being able to try on Vera Wang and no-name Wanda in the same place because if you're going to spring for Vera, you need to know that you actually do like her dresses better than the other stuff. I found that trying on gowns right next to another bride who would *only* put on designer duds was reassuring. I found a dress I loved right away, while she was frustrated limiting herself strictly to designers. Plus, mine cost a fraction of what the ones she tried did. I had to resist the urge to point and laugh.

Another option is shopping at a chain store. There are national chains a la David's Bridal, but most areas have local chains as well. These stores promise a wide selection, but I find that they can be too overwhelming. They remind me of the last scene of *Citizen Kane* but instead of endless statues and ornate knickknacks, there's an endless sea of organza and beading. True, you can find good deals in chains, but there are deals to be found everywhere (more on that later). How-ever, if one-stop-shopping is what you're after, you can't beat the bridal chains.

Department stores often carry bridal sections. Nord-strom, Filene's, and Bergdorf Goodman are just a few. While your experience at each of these places will vary, I feel you should expect just as much personalized attention at depart-ment stores as you'd receive at another bridal salon. Obvi-ously their selection will be more limited than national bridal chains, but if you have a specific dress or designer in mind that's carried in the department store, this is certainly a good bet. You also might check out their non-wedding designer sections. My friend actually got a gorgeous dress in Barneys' cruisewear section.

Then there are designer boutiques, like Carolina Her-rera, of course Vera, Priscilla of Boston, and the like. Usually these salons are located in large cities or the city where that particular designer is located. If you're really into fashion, know you look good in a specific label, or have a couple of favorite designers who also do wedding gowns, it can save a lot of time by starting at one of these stores first.

Personally, I find it's good to shop around. In fact, I rec-ommend making an appointment with about three different salons. Yes, you can walk in off the street at most places and browse, but you should absolutely make an appointment before you try things on. That way, you know you'll have a salesperson devoting time to you. Take a day or two off of work to do this. The store will be so much less crowded dur-ing the day on a weekday than on an evening or weekend, when they'll be bombarded with brides.

A few words of wisdom: I've interviewed countless designers who all say the same thing: Do *not* bring a posse with you to the bridal salon. I know it sounds like a fun-filled, girly bonding experience having all your bridesmaids and mother-in-law sipping champagne and watching you twirl around in frock after lovely frock, oohing and ahhing over the pretty ones and giggling about the hideous ones. But here's the deal: What you consider pretty or hideous is bound to differ from what someone else in your posse thinks is pretty or hideous. You don't want too many opinions thrown your way—they can seriously confuse you. They can have you starting to think that maybe you do really love poufy Glinda-the-Good-Witch sleeves and that that V-neck might be too revealing, even though your cleavage is your favorite asset. So bring *one or two* people whose opinions you trust (and this should include your mom because she'd make you feel too guilty if you didn't).

"I bought a dress with a train for a beach wedding. I knew the train wasn't practical and would end up getting all sandy and dirty, but I didn't expect it to look like I fished it out of the bottom of a litter box."

—Melissa

Before you head to your appointment, be prepared. Bring your favorite strapless bra with you and wear good underwear because people will be watching. Spanx are great to give you that overall "sucking in" effect. Eat well so you have the stamina to endure many changes, but not so well that you'll feel bloated. Also, bring along a bottle of water. While this may sound a bit paranoid, I've witnessed (and, admittedly, *experienced*) some low-blood-sugar- and dehydration-induced shopping meltdowns. The experience can be more overwhelming than you think. You need to prepare for wedding dress shopping as you would an Olympic marathon. The two have more in common than you might think.

WEDDING DRESS CUTS THAT WON'T CUT YOU OFF

- **Ball gown.** Think Beauty and the Beast. This is a dramatic look—perfect if you're marrying in a gilded ballroom or a historic home. But let's face it, it's not ideal for a barefoot beach wedding or one at a chic, modern art gallery. Ball gowns look especially fantastic on curvy women—your waist will look teeny! But if you're petite, you could drown in a dress this voluminous.
- **A-line.** A-line dresses are known as the ones that look good on everyone. They hug curves on top, then flare out in a not-too-big skirt—but big enough to disguise some "hippiness." A pretty a-line dress is very feminine and traditional looking. You can make it work for almost any wedding—choose rich embellishments like silk-satin and Alencon lace for a formal wedding, and maybe a nice jersey material for a casual backyard bash.
- **Sheath.** This is the one for that chic cocktail party. It would work for beach nuptials as well. A slinky sheath is sexy and sophisticated, but it's also best if you've got a slender bod. Since it will cling to your every curve, you don't want to wear a sheath if you're particularly self-conscious about your figure.
- **Mermaid.** A mermaid gown definitely works for beach, but it could fit for almost any type of event. A mermaid is body-hugging down to the knees, then

flares out (yup, like mermaid fins). Beware that it can definitely put some emphasis on those hips.

- **Empire.** This is a good choice for small busted brides. An empire waist falls right below the bust, creating volume up top. The skirt size can vary but usually it's flowy and girly. As with other cuts, the fabric of your empire gown will dictate just how formal the look will be.

FINDING THE PERFECT GUY WAS EASY COMPARED TO FINDING THE PERFECT DRESS

There is no one specific way to find the dress of your dreams. Some brides do a little pre-shopping research, perusing different designers' web pages and tearing pages out of bridal magazines. Others do their research in their very own closets. Look at your dresses—and even your skirts and blouses. Which ones do you wear the most? Which ones best flatter your body type and make you feel confident and drop dead gorgeous? What do they have in common? Pay particular attention to their lines and proportions. What kind of necklines, skirt shapes, and silhouettes do they have? What kind of details do they have and how would you say they express your style? Are they contemporary? Romantic? Slinky? Retro? What you discover can serve as inspiration when you're shopping. Tell your salesperson about your personal tastes and preferences when you get there.

But here comes the contradiction: I've heard *tons* of brides report that they fall in love with a gown that they never even wanted to try on in the first place. These might be the same women who fell in love with a guy they never wanted to go out with in the first place either. What I'm trying to say here is: be open-minded. You absolutely love Empire waist gowns and you wouldn't be caught dead wearing strapless, but try one on just in case. You never know. This is especially true for those who have a specific dress in mind and carry around a picture of it that they tore from *Modern Bride* circa 1997.

In an effort to save time, be as specific as you can with your salesperson. I know I was frustrated buttoning 100 buttons only to find the dress made me look like the Stay-Puffed Marshmallow Man. That's why it's important to tell your sales assistant, "I don't like this because . . ." or "I like the beading detail on the train, but the sweetheart neckline really isn't my thing." Usually, the people who work in the stores try to listen to customers and respond by bringing them things that better fit their tastes. Now, occasionally these same sales associates may bring you something completely different than what you're asking for. If so, just kindly tell them, "No, thank you" (even though you're thinking "There's no way in hell . . .").

THINGS THAT SUCK ABOUT TRYING ON WEDDING DRESSES

- **None of them will fit,** unless you're six foot three and a size 6. Stores usually stock samples in only one size. If you're smaller, you'll be squeezed in with some sort of clamp-type hardware. If you're bigger, sorry my dear. Unless you find a plus size store, you'll have to put the dress on with your bare back showing because you won't be able to zip it—or you might have to do a lot of holding up and imagining. And pretty much everyone will have to stand on a block or platform to let the ultra long dress fall to the floor the way it would for Uma Thurman.

- **The labels will make you feel fat.** Yep, that feels-like-a-6 sample will actually be marked with a 10. To make you feel extra bad about your body, all wedding dresses will be marked about two sizes (give or take) higher than comparable street clothes would be. This size system must have been dreamed up by whoever decided that all brides should wear the most non-slimming dress color there is.

- **There are actually a lot of words for white.** Candlelight. Ivory. Cream. Ecru. I could go on all day. What's the difference? It all varies my manufacturer, so if you're trying to match a dress and a veil, don't go by the name but rather hold the fabrics next to each other.

- **You will fall in love with something out of your price range.** It's inevitable. But don't freak because you can't afford it and it's so amazing. There's plenty more out there that are completely lovely and more reasonable so keep looking.

- **Like and love are very different things.** Chances are, you'll probably find a lot of gowns that are downright pretty, so how do you actually make a decision? Most brides report that there was "just something" about their dress that made it stand out from the crowd. I hate to be so vague, but keep browsing until you find something with a *je ne sais quoi*. That will be the one worth the dough.

YOU GET WHAT YOU PAY FOR . . . OR DO YOU?

An awful comedian might ask, what's the difference between
a dress from the chain store's $99 rack and a $7,000 designer
beauty? About $6,000 (bad um dum)! Actually, it's the com-
bination of several things. For one, a dress that's been put on
the $99 rack has probably been left behind from last season
or last year. For another, it might be only available in that
size, purchased right off the rack (not ordered in your specific size or color, like a new dress would be). It might also
be sold "as is," meaning it has a snag or a stain or some other
flaw that you'll be stuck with if you purchase it—because
you won't be allowed to return it.

The $99 dress may have originally cost anywhere from
$400 to $1,000. A wedding dress in this price range may be
on the affordable side for several reasons. It could be a slinky,
simple style, without a ton of layers of fabric or beading or
embroidery and thus took less resources and manpower to
make. It could have been mass produced in a country with
cheap labor where the stitching and details were created by
machine. Some of the details might not be luxurious. For
example, you might have buttons for show but a zipper that
actually fastens the dress, or perhaps the lace is pretty but
not very finely detailed.

The $7,000 dress, on the other hand, may be created
to order, just for you. This is normally the case for couture
gowns. In other words, instead of producing a bunch of
size 8 dresses in hopes that someone will order them, the
designer will take your order *then* make a dress for your measurements (it will still need altering, though). It may have a
lot of layers of fabric and be made of an expensive, luxurious
material instead of a cheap, rough fabric that feels itchy and

has weird reflective properties. Details may be hand-stitched or made of gossamer-thin, intricate lace. Designer dresses are often made in the United States or Italy or somewhere where *artisans* earn higher wages than the seamstresses who work on the Jaclyn Smith collection at K-mart (not that there's anything *wrong* with Jaclyn or K-mart). A lot of time and energy have gone into the design and craftsmanship of a $7,000 dress. The $99 dress may have simply been made as a copy, or a composite of features of several different designer dresses (think of those cheap knockoffs that magically appear in the mall after the Oscars).

Now, that doesn't mean that you can't find a good quality dress for less. It just may have to be from last year's collection, bought at a sample sale, or simply a very minimalist style, without all the crystals and beading and underskirt netting. Or you may have to get a bit creative with where and how you're shopping. Don't know how? Well I've got some ideas for you.

Dress For Less

If you don't have the funds for a pricy dress (or would rather spend it on a year's worth of groceries), there are some tricks of the wedding dress trade. But be warned: these options have risks.

The Sample Sale. Fashionistas in big cities are quite familiar with sample sales. They're what happen when the designer or a store needs to unload some inventory. Often you're able to get a designer dress for up to 75 percent off. However, you might have to wait in line to get in and then literally fight off a crowd of brides all desperate for a good deal as well. When I first got engaged, I found myself at a Vera Wang sample sale that was very, very scary. I think it would make a great scene for the next *Saw* movie. Sizes and colors will most likely be extremely limited, and some dresses will be torn, dirty, or flawed. And there are no refunds, so be careful! If you fall in love with a dress with a stain, you'll have to take your chances that it'll come out—or else you'll need to strategically attach a brooch to it.

Internet Stores. Some bridal shops have gone to the great lengths of taking labels out of their sample dresses so that you can't go on the Internet and find out if the dress is available for less from someone else. Seriously. So if you're able to do it, you might be tempted to try. The problem with the Internet is that often you're putting trust in a seller that you know nothing about rather than a retail store that answers to your community, the Better Business Bureau, and the dress designer or manufacturer. So be very, very careful. You're investing a lot of money and emotion into this dress—don't trust just anyone who comes up in a Google search.

I'm *really* not a fan of buying a dress sight unseen off the Internet. Like me, you've probably ordered an outfit from a catalog or website that didn't look nearly as good in person as it did on the model in the photo. Is this something you want to happen with your wedding gown? Nay, I say! If you're brave, only do this if you'll be allowed to return the gown for a full refund, and also be aware that many of these sites charge restocking fees.

Consignment Shops. There are some really lovely consignment shops that sell used dresses—some are even nonprofits that donate their earnings to charity. If you don't mind wearing something that someone else has (some people think a used dress could carry bad luck), you can go that route. Be sure you inspect your used dress very carefully before purchasing. Make sure there are no discolorations, snags, or other flaws. Beware that the older the fabric, the more difficult (and possibly damaging) it will be to clean. If you like the old-fashioned look, consider wearing your mom's or grandmother's dress instead—that can carry more sentimental meaning (although I guess if they're divorced, this dress might not have the best of luck either). Extra bonus: Mom's dress is *free*.

eBay, Craigslist, and the Like. I *really* don't love the idea of buying a *used* dress online—it's a double whammy with all the cons of buying a used dress and of buying online combined. If you see something you think you'll love on eBay though, be sure to check the seller's ratings, ask lots of questions, ask for a return policy, and order it with plenty of time (and extra money) to devise a plan B if it doesn't work out.

Off the Rack Sales. In the corner of your bridal salon, there may be a sale section of "off-the-rack" dresses. These are leftover from past seasons and are usually also sold "as is." What you see is what you get, so look closely—maybe some beading is missing, or there's a rip in the seam. Again, ask about the return policy and if you can live with it, and fit into it, feel free to fall for one of these gowns.

Stores You Might Not Have Thought Of. J. Crew, Target.com, JCPenney, and other surprising sellers carry wedding dresses. The J. Crew selection is particularly simple and elegant.

The Non-Wedding Route. Who says your wedding dress has to be made specifically for a bride? Perhaps you find a really pretty evening gown or slip dress available in white or ivory. Or even a hip bridesmaid gown that can be ordered in white. And who the hell said it has to be white anyhow? Prefer another color? Go for it! A non-bridal gown most likely will not be elaborate or intricate but it will probably be much more reasonably priced. And still beautiful! I've never heard anyone say, "The bride's dress was pretty but it didn't have top-to-bottom beading. For shame!"

DECISION MADE! NOW WHAT?

Once you've decided on your gown, you'll have to order it. Plan to do this at least six months before the wedding if you want to avoid paying rush fees. But before you order, the salesperson will have to perform the most traumatic part of the dress buying ordeal: she'll have you strip down to your skivvies and take your measurements (cue frightening *Psycho*-type music)! Trust me, as scary as this sounds, it's way better than her just taking your word for it . . . we all tend to fudge the numbers a little bit (just look at the weight on your driver's license).

"I didn't have a typical wedding dress. I donned a heavily beaded Indian lenga which is a big skirt and top that looks similar to a saree. The beads scratched the hell out of my arms, my exposed waist, and any skin that wasn't covered. I spent my honeymoon dressed in Band-Aids."

—Rabia

The gown will be ordered using what's proportionally your largest size. For example, if you've got big boobs and tiny waist (lucky you!), your bust size will be used as the determiner. If you're border line, the salesperson will suggest you order a size up. With all this in mind—and knowing that wedding dress sizes are wonky—I strongly suggest you don't take the number she writes down on the order form personally. In fact, I suggest you treat it like a solar eclipse and don't look directly at it. This will prevent you from shouting, "But I've never worn that size in my whole damn life!" Also resist saying that you plan to lose weight before the big day so you *must* have a smaller size for motivational purposes. This might seem like a good idea but it is actually a very, very bad idea. I'm not saying you can't lose weight. You *can*. I'm saying that it's seven bazillion times easier—and cheaper—to take a gown in rather than let it out. Imagine trying to order the exact same fabric direct from the manufacturer and asking a seamstress to deconstruct the gown and put it back together with the extra fabric. I know someone who had this done to a bridesmaid dress and it was a whole lotta complicated. It's even more complicated for a wedding dress.

When you place your order, be sure you know exactly when to expect the gown to arrive. Can the store guarantee it by a certain date? You will need to have it in your possession with plenty of time to have at least two fittings with a seamstress before your wedding date. You'll also be required to make a deposit. In most cases, this *should not* be the full amount of the dress's cost. Even if you have all the money, resist the urge to plunk it down. Just pay what's required for the deposit. That way, if there's any sort of problem with shipping, manufacturing, or anything else, you've got a backup budget. Believe me, things happen.

Nip/Tuck

Alterations are vitally important to your whole bridal fashion package. The better your dress fits you, the better you'll look in it. You don't necessarily have to get this done at the store where you bought your dress, but sometimes you'll get a discount if you do (same holds true for accessories). You'll need at least two sessions with the seamstress for alterations. The first should be shortly after the gown comes in, and the second should be a couple weeks before the wedding day—allowing enough time for your seamstress to get everything done. If you're planning on losing weight, or you tend to fluctuate, it's best to schedule one or two additional sessions, and make the final one as close to the date as possible. This will give you extra opportunities for fine tuning.

"My seamstress decided to add tulle to the skirt for fullness, so she pinned it in with hundreds of needles. When I put on the dress just before I walked down the aisle, I painfully discovered all the pins were still in the dress! She'd forgotten to actually sew in the tulle!"

—Christina

We've all seen *Dancing with the Stars* and know the miracles a seamstress can work with a needle, thread, and chicken cutlet bra inserts, so ask yours what she can do to make your dress look—and perform—its best. She may be able to sew in extra support so you don't have to worry about any additional underthingies. She may even be able to give you a little extra oomph up top. She may add undetectable hooks for bustling your train or resituate beading or lace to properly disguise flaws or any hemming she's had to do.

For each fitting, make sure you bring the *actual* shoes you plan to wear, as well as any special underthings like a bustier or Spanx (a bride's best friend!). This will allow your seamstress to make perfect calculations and will let you see exactly how the gown hugs your body. While you're there, walk in the dress. Sit in it. Dance in it. Be sure you'll be able to move comfortably and that you like how much cleavage (or lack thereof) shows from every angle. If you go strapless, you don't want to be constantly pulling your dress up, so make sure the bodice is snug enough.

Also, bring along the jewelry you're planning to wear, and the veil and headpiece too (with the tags still on them if anything's returnable). Make sure the whole ensemble looks the way you want it to. Sometimes you have your heart set on wearing a certain necklace but it doesn't look quite right with the dress's neckline. Or maybe it's too much with the headpiece and veil, too, and you opt for something daintier—or no necklace at all. Usually an elaborate dress doesn't need much in the way of accessories.

When the final alterations are complete and you pick up your gown, try it on one last time in the store to make sure it fits properly. Once again, move around in it, sit in it, dance in it. Look closely at the dress, making sure it looks exactly the way you want from every angle and that the seamstress has performed all the services you've requested.

Take it home and store it somewhere safe, dry, and temperature regulated. Then, at the wedding, keep it the hell away from any guests drinking cranberry juice and vodka on the dance floor at your reception. You will be photographed in it a thousand times that day, and this dress may be something you'll only wear once—but that only means publicly. You'll still be able to put it on many times to come. My favorite is when my guy is out of town on a business trip and I have a pint of Ben and Jerry's in my hand. Don't judge.

CHAPTER 5

The Friends and Family Plan of Attack

Did you ever see The Exorcist? Remember how the little possessed girl's head turned around 180 degrees? The first time I saw it, it gave me chills. Now it just reminds me of wedding planning. That's because as soon as a woman says, "Yes, I'll marry you" everything starts turning 180 degrees. Pleasant, loving moms become psycho and controlling. Laid-back supportive friends turn into selfish, evil bridesmaids. And getting along with your future in-laws can be harder to deal with than the pea-soup projectile vomiting scene.

So how do you handle these newly complicated relationships—on top of those that are already complicated, like divorced parents, jealous siblings, or soon to be step-children? Well, you've got to know what to expect, make the right strategies to cope and, well, remember that you really do like your best friend even though she's throwing a temper tantrum about open-toed shoes.

Planning your wedding is not only stressful for you and your fiancé, but it can also be incredibly emotional for people you love and adore. And when those people are stressed, the stress boomerang comes back at you with full force and is aimed directly at your head! Nonetheless, there are ways to duck and cover, and knowing what to expect is always a good place to start.

MOMZILLA

Your mom loves you, even when she acts crazy. Remember that. You know those "stage moms" you hear about and watch on cable TV? The ones who live their dreams through their children, barking out orders at every audition, forcing them to put in fake teeth and get spray tans at the pageants? Those mothers are pretty insane, eh? Well, hold on tight, sister, because your mom might be offered her own cable TV show in the not-too-distant future.

This "stage mom" phenomenon is an all-too-familiar problem with brides-to-be. Mom becomes ridiculously excited about planning your wedding, as if it was her big moment. And to her, it is. Maybe she's being obvious about it, butting in on your meeting with the florist and making the big decisions before you get the chance to utter your opinion. And then you're left wondering how you ended up with a Neil Diamond playlist for your reception. Or maybe she's being more subtle, letting you make your own choices but then promptly putting them down. It really does suck to hear Mom badmouth everything you were initially excited about, from the simple-yet-chic lantern centerpieces to the little cheddar sliders you want to serve at the cocktail hour (c'mon Mom, who doesn't like mini *cheeseburgers*? They're cute—not trashy.). I learned to simply smile and change the subject when my mom pooh-poohed my decisions. I strongly advise you to do the same.

It's a difficult balance. You want a supportive advisor with you to help you plan your wedding. We've already established that no one, no matter how Type-A they are, should tackle this challenge alone. But you don't want that someone who's sitting in the passenger seat to decide to throw you in the trunk. Weddings are your chance to let your personality shine, to have a big party that's all about you and your future hubby, and reflect your personality and taste—not Mommy's.

This dilemma becomes far more complicated if Mom is contributing financially to your wedding. In this case, you do owe her some respect and that means taking her suggestions seriously. You don't want to piss her off, hurt your relationship, or worse, risk her cutting off the money supply. I know you feel like telling her off and running the other way, but there are better ways to deal with an overbearing mom:

Listen to Mom without immediately disregarding her opinions. Often the problem stems from a generation gap. When my mom nixed my dream of colorful invitations in lieu of simple black-and-white flat card invites, it was because that style was long considered the signal of a formal celebration. But times have changed, and couples are now picking a variety of colors and styles of invitations. Imagine that you're in love with a gorgeous red floral scheme and your mom is just as negative about it as mine was. Think hard and objectively about the decision. Is Mom right, or is the invitation formal enough for the wedding you're planning? If you're still set on your choice, explain to her nicely where you're coming from.

Bring in the experts. If she's still not budging, have the salesclerk reassure her that your choice is right. Or ask your wedding planner to do the honors. That alone may be worth the price of hiring her! Sometimes people respond when they hear things from a neutral third party—and as much as we'd like our mothers to respect our opinions, sometimes they *believe* they know better than their little girls.

Make efforts to communicate effectively with Mom. Have a sit-down during a calm moment and be direct. Run down all the tasks you have left on your to-do list. Outline exactly what you'd like her help with and exactly what you'd prefer to handle on your own. If she's footing the bill, she might give you limits on certain things—budget-wise and decision-wise. My mom doesn't care for halter bridal gowns, so since she was paying for my dress, I made a deal to omit them from my options—in fact, it made narrowing down dress choices even easier.

Ask your mom if *her* mother helped plan her wedding and how it went. If you're lucky, she'll recount how her own mother became overbearing and insisted on things she didn't like. That slap in the face of reality might hold up a mirror to her own behavior.

Mom still won't budge? Order the invites anyhow and put them on *your* tab. She really can't argue too much when you're paying, and when it's something you're that passionate about.

If you've tried talking with your mom and she is still controlling, it's best to cut the satin apron strings and plan most of the wedding without her. Do your own research, find your own vendors. Ask a sister or trusted friend for help. Hire a wedding planner or a personal concierge service to help you out with the extra stuff. Off the bat, you're setting the precedent that this is the way it's going to be from here on out. Remember that moms love this wedding crap, so occasionally ask for her opinion. Maybe you've found two dresses you love and can have her make the final decision. Or, if you found the dress all on your own, bring mom to the salon to see it—not approve it—and have her help you with the accessories. Moms seriously eat up bridal salons, so don't deny her this big moment! Even the most overbearing mom can be involved without taking over. It will make you both feel good.

TEN WAYS TO THANK MOM FOR HER HELP
(No matter how much you two clashed, she deserves it!)

1. **Make a toast.** During the reception, you and New Hubs can get up and say cheers to everyone who helped you out. Mention Mom by name and say that you couldn't have done it without her.
2. **Put it in the program.** Couples often include a sweet note thanking loved ones in their ceremony program. This is nice, in addition to a more grand gesture.
3. **Treat her to ice cream.** Or a martini. Or whatever else she loves. During this hectic time, when it seems like everything you do together is wrapped up in wedding planning, do something that's not. Dinner, shopping, pedicures, gelato, whatever!
4. **Take her dress shopping.** Devote a day—or several—to shopping for the perfect mother-of-the-bride dress. Don't do this in conjunction with your or your bridesmaids' dresses. This time, it's all about Mom.
5. **Plan special flowers.** Okay, so maybe you don't want to play favorites, but make Mom's wedding day flowers a bit different than your future mother-in-

law's. Figure out what will look best with her dress, or ask her what style she prefers. (I didn't know that my mom wanted a wrist corsage instead of a pin until she told me.) Maybe she loves lilies and your fiancé's mama is mad about roses. This way, they each can have something that makes them feel special.

6. **Pay tribute to her and Dad.** If your parents are together, ask the band to play their song at your reception. Hell, even if Mom has a new husband or boyfriend, you can still do this for them. They'll totally appreciate the thought—and enjoy the dance!

7. **Walk the aisle with Mom.** Who says that Dad's the only one who can escort the bride at the ceremony? In some cultures, both parents walk with the bride. If your father has passed away or is out of the picture, it's more than appropriate to have Mom do the honors. Or, Dad can walk you halfway down the aisle, then you can meet Mom for the rest of the walk.

8. **Buy a sentimental gift.** It's customary for the bride and groom to give their parents gifts. You can present them at the rehearsal dinner or on the morning of the wedding. Choose something sentimental, like a beautiful framed photo of Mom with you as a baby, or a piece of jewelry engraved with a heartfelt message.

9. **Plan a girls' trip.** I know there's a lot going on, so you might not be able to put all the details in place just yet, but tell Mom that the next trip you take after your honeymoon will be a girls' vacation with her. Go wine tasting or have a spa weekend.

10. **Write a thank-you note.** Seriously, this is the best way to thank just about anyone! Remember that the note you write to Mom should definitely come from the heart.

DIVORCE IS A DIRTY WORD

If you thought your parents' divorce was tough when you were going through it, wait until you have to plan your wedding around it. My parents are still together, but my husband's mother and step-father decided to split a few months before our big day. Even though everyone made nicey-nice at the wedding, just knowing they'd split up made things super awkward and made some logistics quite complicated. I was afraid to include parents in the wedding party announcements at the reception, and I decided not to display family wedding photos, even though I love when couples do that! Also, formal "family photos" after the ceremony took close to a year, with all the sets of parents (three) and grandparents (five) my husband has. Since about 50 percent of marriages end in divorce, 50 percent of couples who plan weddings probably end up with a similar amount of extra crap to deal with.

Money

First up is dealing with money. Let's say your mom has more of it than your dad. Dad insists that he match Mom in order to compete, but he can't really afford it because he has his "new" family to support. Or one parent refuses to pay because the other is making a killing in the alimony settlement. Or one offers and the other doesn't—should you ask? Money is complicated enough to deal with when you're planning a wedding without throwing divorce in the mix. You become the well-meaning carrier pigeon who must flit around through knife-worthy tension from party to party, trying not to piss anyone off.

Whether your parents divorced two months ago or twenty years ago, it'll still be difficult. Go to each party in question and ask them if they would like to contribute to the wedding. If they do, ask them what they feel comfortable giving. Whether the number is big or small, or if they say yes or no, thank them. Then, no matter what you do, don't reveal any numbers to either party. If they ask how much the other parent is giving, change the subject or tell them you don't know the exact figure yet. The money given to a couple to plan their wedding is not directly proportional to the amount of love a parent has for a child—but people forget that sometimes. Don't let them forget that, and don't forget that yourself.

Invitations

If there's divorce in your family, it may take you longer to compose your invitations than it took Beethoven to compose an entire symphony. That's because divorces and remarriages make for more names to include or exclude and decisions about which names go in which order. A once short list of Mom and Dad will now read more like a movie's closing credits. Before you start freaking out about how many "parents" you have to mention and order invitations that unroll like Santa's naughty list, remember to focus. Ask yourself, who is hosting this wedding? If it's you and your groom, and your families aren't playing a large financial role, then something like this is the answer to your wording prayers:

> Francine Anne Lewis
>
> and John Randall Scott
>
> request the pleasure of your company at the celebration of their marriage

However, any large sum of money donated to the celebration should probably be acknowledged. Sometimes, instead of listing names, a general, all-parent-encompassing phrasing is the way to go. Like this:

> Together with their parents
>
> Francine Anne Lewis
>
> and John Randall Scott
>
> request the pleasure of your company at the celebration of their marriage

Some parents won't care whether they're mentioned in the wedding invitation at all, in which case you can get away with:

> The honor of your presence
>
> is requested at the marriage of
>
> Francine Anne Lewis
>
> and John Randall Scott

But others might be offended if they're not mentioned. And I get it—it's not that they're being selfish. It's just that this invitation will be going out to their family and friends too, and they're taking pride in your day. Okay, maybe they're taking some credit, too. But you might as well let them. Your invitation may read something like this, if Mom and Dad are divorced and Dad remarried.

> Mr. and Mrs. Christopher Lewis
>
> Ms. Rachel Prince
>
> request the pleasure of your company at
> the marriage of their daughter
>
> Francine Anne Lewis
>
> to John Randall Scott

Tread lightly because some people are really into etiquette, and they may pay particular attention to whom you mention first, since that's supposed to be the most recognized parent. I know I'm a former bridal magazine editor and I'm supposed to be big on proper etiquette, but I'm so not. I think it's antiquated and not flexible enough for the special circumstances that are part of today's society. That said, when it comes to weddings, *other* people are still conscious of etiquette and I've learned that it's important to respect that.

With this invitation wording, you're paying homage to the people who are contributing to your wedding. Mention the person who's contributing the most first. You may decide that "contributing the most" isn't just a matter of money. Sure, your dad might be handing over the big bucks, but your mom has given what she can, *and* has taken time off work, flown in to stay with you, painstakingly helped you choose a menu, bridesmaids' dresses, and the perfect white lace to wrap around your bouquet of calla lilies, plus calmed you down through some nervous mood swings and tantrums. So, in that respect, feel free to give her top billing if you feel it's right.

Remember, you don't *have* to mention everyone who gives you money on your wedding invitation, just whomever you consider the "hosts." But, if someone is helping you out, they probably deserve it, so consider it. And if one of those people is that evil bitch you must call a step-mother, maybe the "together with their parents" route is the way to go.

Walking Down the Aisle

The repercussions of a divorce will come into play on the wedding day too. Should Dad really be the one walking you down the aisle when your step-father is the one who raised you? What if you don't have a dad, only a step-dad that you despise? What if you love both dads wholly and completely? Luckily there are many ways to play this game.

These days, it's perfectly acceptable to have one dad walk you halfway, then hand you off to the other dad, who gives you away. Or you can have your mother walk you down if she's the one who played the greatest role in your life or if you don't like your step-dad. Brothers and uncles are great substitutes as well. Or you can walk alone. Or you and your groom can walk together—that can be very symbolic if you've been a couple for a long time. The point is, anyone can walk you down the aisle, so choose someone who's important to you. If you feel like you'll hurt someone by omitting them from the ceremony, you can thank them in the written ceremony programs or during a speech at the rehearsal dinner or reception.

The Seating Chart

The traditional way to seat parents during the ceremony is to have the bride and groom's parents in the first row (on each side of the church). But, when you're dealing with divorced parents, maybe it's best to seat them at totally different weddings! Depending on how well they get along, you can try putting whoever raised you, with their spouse and your siblings, in the front row, with the other parent in the second. Not so amicable? Use your grandparents as a buffer in row two and put the other parent in row three. Capisce? If your parents can be civil to each other, and their new spouses are understanding, you can have your parents sit together in the front with their kids behind them. Or you can seat them alphabetically by middle names. Whatever works best for you and causes the least amount of strife (no matter what you do, there will be some strife).

As if ceremony seating isn't complex enough, you'll have to work out a way to separate divorced relatives at the reception as well. Instead of having one VIP table with your parents, siblings, and grandparents, you'll need to create a few extra VIP tables with different parts of the family. The key is to place them close to the two of you so they feel like VIPs, but not close to each other where they'll be tempted to hire a hit man. If you're afraid one set of parents will feel slighted because they don't get to sit with you at the reception, have a sweetheart table for two. Yup, sit with your fiancé and only your fiancé. Then no one can get jealous because their ex dines with you and they don't.

Yes, dealing with divorced parents is never pretty. If your parents get upset, remind them that they chose to get divorced and there are consequences to their actions. You had to deal with being schlepped from house to house as a kid, and they have to deal with this!

The Dance

The "dad" confusion continues to cause stress at the reception when it's time for the traditional dance with your father. Again, be flexible. You can dance with one dad, then halfway through, the other can cut in. Or you can dance with Mom or your brother instead. Or your step-dad, as long as your father won't be totally offended by this (or won't pretend that he isn't). If the whole thing is too sticky or weird, it's best not to even partake in this tradition. I guarantee your guests won't miss it—they'll be more interested in hitting the dance floor themselves than watching a bunch of cheesy "spotlight" dances. Plus, isn't the dance (as well as the walking down the aisle thing) an antiquated concept? Marriages in our society are no longer transfer of property transactions. You are not "owned" by your father who will hand you to your groom along with a fatted calf and a handful of young chickens.

MEETING THE FOCKERS

"Future mother-in-law." These four words strike as much panic in women as "Oops, the condom broke." The reason why future mother-in-laws (or monster-in-laws as they're known in the wedding biz) are so scary has something to do with the unique relationship guys have with their moms. To the guys, Mom is the ultimate do-no-wrong woman. To the moms, their little boy is their baby, and you're the evil lady who's taking him away and disagreeing with do-no-wrong mom. You can easily be stuck between a rock and a hard-to-please woman.

> **"My dad wasn't living with his second wife at the time of our wedding and he wouldn't tell me whether he was bringing her or his new girlfriend to the event. I was so disgusted, I ended up putting him at the kiddie table."**
>
> **—Randi**

To cap it off, your future mother-in-law might not be the only tough cookie to crumble in your soon-to-be new family. His siblings can be cold toward you. His dad can be stoic or egotistical. It can even be awkward to meet his grandma who adored your fiancé 's ex-girlfriend and secretly hoped they'd get back together.

If you don't live near your future in-laws or you haven't been dating a long time, the engagement period might be the first time you meet your future family. If this is true, you don't get the luxury of a meet-and-greet warm up period. You have to hit the relationship ground running, knowing full well that you all have to love each other (or pretend that you do) from this day forward. Yes, for better or worse, richer or poorer, these are the people you'll be spending holidays with, sending birthday gifts to, and trying not to let get between you and your husband.

While they might seem weird to you, you have to keep in mind you might seem weird to them too. But weird or not, you're suddenly family and it's important that you extend an olive branch, even if they're being rude or standoffish. Make a date to have lunch with his mom one on one. Take Grandma and future sister-in-laws shopping or to tea. Make an extra effort—without making a big deal about doing it. Show them how wonderful it will be to have you as an in-law.

One common problem is when his family has different traditions, religious beliefs, or general way of life than yours. You may not support their love of hunting or their political party. But they may not be supportive of your tattoos, your ambitious career, or your taste in micro-miniskirts. So they might be unreasonable about accepting you. Before you start name-calling and driving past their house in the middle of the night to throw a bag of dog poo on their porch, try to be the bigger person. Show interest in your fiancé's family traditions by asking his parents about them. Listen to their old stories. Explain how you'd like to merge both of your cultures and beliefs in your newlywed home. Get creative—suggest you have both a Christmas tree and a menorah. It's important that you have some ideas and verbalize them.

Say you're trying hard with the in-laws (or should we call them outlaws?) and they're still acting like babies, or they do or say something that's insensitive, hurtful, or completely ridiculous. My friend Amie's mother-in-law had a fit when she decided to upgrade the liquor choices at her reception—even though Amie's mom was going to pay for it, not her! She said some very nasty, hurtful things to Amie. This is where you would take a deep breath and call on your fiancé. I know that guys would rather peel off their skin than get between you and their mothers, but he needs to learn to stand up for you. Conflicts like this won't stop at the wedding, and your fiancé needs to know that you're the family he needs to put first. It's important.

Eventually, everyone's going to have to find a way to make peace with the new family you're creating. It could be that you have to bite your tongue when certain issues are brought up or there might always be a big rift between you and your in-laws. And that's totally okay, so long as you don't host any family dinner parties where steak knives are involved.

TWISTED SISTER

Your relationship with your siblings can get strained during your wedding planning. Not so much with your brothers, who don't normally give a rat's ass about weddings or have deep seeded emotional issues to deal with. Just serve them a great steak at the reception and choose a bridesmaid dress with deep cleavage and they're good to go. Sisters, however, are a whole different story. No matter how close the two of you are going into a wedding, you can come out the other side with lifelong resentments.

"As soon as I got engaged, my sister started dating a guy who had more tattoos than brain cells and kept dissing my wedding. It reminded me of when we were kids and she'd act out to get negative attention."

—Brianne

The problems are often caused by a jealousy thing. All your lives, you and your sister have been compared to each other—maybe even competed against each other—and now you're the one who's the center of attention. And if you're getting married before your older sister does, it's the sister equivalent of getting kicked in the balls. Don't expect Sis to be 100 percent supportive of your wedding if this is the case. In fact, she's liable to criticize your decisions, distance herself from you, throw tantrums like when you were eight and she divided your room in half with masking tape, or stick to more passive aggressive coping methods. While it may be more satisfying to yell and tell your sister where she can shove it, it's far better for your relationship if you:

- **Spend time with her doing non-wedding things**. When you're wrapped up in wedding planning, it's hard not to talk about your nuptials all the time. But give Sis a break and talk about—and do—something completely different.

- **Give your sister a special role**. Even if you don't like your sister as much as you like your best friend (hey, we're being honest here), your sister will feel cheated if you ask your best friend to be MOH instead. If you think your sister isn't up for the challenge, have co-MOHs, or a married friend can be the matron of honor and your sister can be maid of honor.

- **Have her help making decisions**. Maybe your sister feels that you're focusing so much time on your wedding and fiancé that she's second fiddle. Help her feel important by asking for her opinion about china patterns and veil styles. However, this plan will certainly backfire if you don't like your sister's taste and keep choosing the opposite of what she suggests or if your sister is tired of hearing about the wedding, so make an educated decision.

- **Hook her up**. If there's a really hot groomsman, make sure your single sister gets paired with him for walking the aisle and dancing. Then, talk him up so she starts to look forward to the wedding.
- **Make Mom the mediator**. It worked when she taped your room in half and it can work now too. Have one of your parents talk to your sister about why she should let go of her crazy resentment and be happy for you.

A WEDDING CAN BE A TRUE TEST OF FRIENDSHIP

I can't even count the number of women who told me they lost longtime friends while planning their wedding. The problems that can happen with friends are insanely similar to those you encounter with sisters, except that sisters have the rest of the family to answer to, as well as the possibility of one day needing your kidney, so they probably won't fall out of your life completely.

If the issues with your friends are mainly a product of them being jealous that you're getting married and they're not, deal with it similarly to how you would a sister (except the whole siccing mom on her thing.) But sometimes, friends' jealousy is a bit different. It's not that they want to be getting married, they just don't want to be replaced by the groom as the most important "friend" in your life. Often friends see you planning a wedding and begin to see the end of Martini-and-Monopoly Mondays and other fun girl stuff. If this is the case, the best thing you can do is sit your friend down and talk to her about it. Tell her how excited you are about getting married and how you always want to be as close as you two are now. Plan for martinis and Monopoly next Monday, as well as the one after that—and hold true to your plan. Because as much as you *tell* your pal that things won't change between you and her once you're married, showing her is much more effective.

> "At one wedding, I heard the bride's so-called best friend say, 'Weddings just make me depressed.' Some people can't be happy for other people, and that's just plain wrong."
>
> —Sarah

Now take a good look in the mirror. Could your sulky friend be justified in her feelings? Have you been acting like a spoiled brat? Have you been making your wedding the priority and letting your friendship fall by the wayside? Do you expect her to be as absorbed in the wedding as you are? Are you asking her to shell out a hell of a lot of money that isn't really necessary? If you weren't sure how to answer any of those questions, I suggest you change your behavior. Pronto.

I know, I know: you're getting married. All you need is love. Blah blah blah. But having friends is also nice. And as we get older, it gets harder to make them. You push your friends away now, and you might not end up with any left. And while your guy sure is cute, he probably doesn't have anything significant to add about what's happening on *Grey's Anatomy* and whether or not gladiator sandals are flattering. And let's face it: this stuff is important to discuss.

Chapter 6

It Takes a Village of Vendors to Throw a Wedding

Searching for wedding vendors is like digging through supermarket tomatoes in the middle of winter. You'll have to search through all the dull, tasteless ones in hopes of finding even one that will shine. Like the tomatoes, there are plenty of vendors to choose from. More than you'll ever need. The trick is to find a vendor that's experienced, easy to work with, listens to what you want, doesn't talk you into what you don't want, is reliable, and is someone you can afford. It may be harder to find a good vendor than to find a good man!

A vendor can make or break your wedding day. It can mean the difference between a gorgeous, multi-tiered cake, or a dry one held up by toothpicks. It can mean the difference between portraits that look like they belong in a fashion magazine, or photos that look like mugshots on the FBI Most Wanted list. Yes, vendors are important. And because you hope this is the last wedding you'll ever have to plan, you only get this one chance. So take a deep breath and grab your checkbook, because we're going shopping for vendors!

WHAT DO YOU MEAN YOU'RE BOOKED ALREADY?

You've heard the horror stories about how long it takes to plan a wedding. Popular venues get booked years in advance. Well-known vendors get hired out quickly as well. In fact, if you've always dreamt of a spring wedding at a well-known hotel, you should have booked it when your guy asked you out on a first date.

Every bride's timeline is different (your priorities will help you figure out your own schedule) but in general, here's how long before the wedding I recommend you secure your vendors:

- **Wedding planner:** 9–12 months
- **Ceremony and reception sites:** 9–12 months
- **Caterer:** 9–10 months
- **Officiant:** 9–10 months
- **Photographer:** 7–9 months
- **DJ or band:** 7–9 months
- **Florist:** 6–8 months
- **Invitations:** 6–8 months
- **Cake baker:** 6–8 months
- **Videographer:** 5–7 months
- **Transportation:** 2–4 months

If you're rushing to get married because you can't wait to start your lives together (code for "Oops! I got knocked up!"), then you'll need to be more flexible. Think a park wedding instead of the Four Seasons. Have your second cousin get ordained on the Internet instead of using a large church's minister. No matter how brief a timeframe you get to plan your wedding, you'll still have a lifetime of memories to enjoy.

HOW TO FIND YOUR SOUL-VENDOR

As a wedding writer, I've asked many "experts" for their advice on finding, meeting, and working with just about every type of wedding vendor, from stationers to florists. While each vendor has their own set of questions to ask and considerations to make, there are some universal truths. With any type of wedding vendor, you need to narrow down the choices from the very beginning. To do this, it's best to start with personal recommendations. Family members and friends whose weddings you enjoyed or whose style you like are an excellent place to start. As tempting as it is to just Google "florists in the Bay Area," you'll be overwhelmed by the number of choices and would have to postpone your wedding until Spring of 2040 to go through them all.

If you can only find one good recommendation, that's fine. In fact, it may be all you need since it could start a domino effect of vendor recommendations. Photographers have attended a lot of weddings and most likely know some good bands. Site managers have worked with different florists and have a solid idea of who delivers pretty arrangements and who is reliable.

If, however, you can't find even one vendor that comes personally recommended, you have no choice but to surf the web. But instead of relying solely on Google, use a website such as Yelp.com or Citysearch.com that offer reviews from past clients. Chances are, many positive reviews translate to a great vendor. (Some sites like TheKnot.com and magazines like *Brides* give out vendor awards, but look closely at the fine print. Do you think the vendor received the reward because they're an advertiser? Are they really amazing, but unaffordable for anyone who isn't a Trump?)

The next step is to check out the vendor's website or ads. If you find them attractive and organized, with lovely photos of their work, they're worth considering. If there are misspellings, a lack of information, or unprofessional or mediocre images, cross them off your list. You'll be amazed at how much you can learn from this first impression. Once the list if made, it's a good idea to check with the Better Business Bureau to see if they have any complaints from prior clients. Look up your local BBB office in the Yellow Pages and call them, or do a search at bbb.org.

Now that you've got your list finalized, call the vendors and ask if they're available on your wedding date. If so, set up an appointment and meet with them. When you do, don't make the rookie mistake of acting shy or playing a people pleaser. Remember, no matter what your job title is in the real world, you're the boss of your wedding (or co-boss if your fiancé, mother, or God forbid, mother-in-law wants to be in on the action). Find out if they're qualified and affordable. Tell them exactly what you're looking for and ask their advice on things you're not. I'd forgo asking for recommendations since, unless they're total buffoons, they'll only supply you with a list of clients who will give them a thumbs up. This is where Yelp.com and Citysearch .com will come into play.

Most importantly, check out their previous work. A florist will have pictures of arrangements they've created. A band will have recordings of their songs—they might even play for you live. I once interviewed an arrogant videographer who pooh-poohed wedding writers who tell brides to watch potential videographers' videos to get an idea of their work. He claimed that he captures each individual wedding, so what he can do for you will be different from what he's done for other couples in the past. I told him that couples who watch his videos *can* get an idea of the video and sound quality, editing techniques, and overall presentation his company offers. For someone to plunk down what could be a down payment on a new car to reserve his services sight unseen would be sort of ridiculous, don't you think?

Talent isn't the only thing you should look for in a vendor. Personality is important too. It may be more important in, say, a photographer who'll be following you around for your entire wedding day than the cake baker who will simply drop off the cake and high tail it outta there. But then again, even the baker will need to listen to your ideas, articulate his suggestions, and plan out the logistics with you. So, talent first, personality second, because even if you click with someone, if they can't do a good job, then you're totally screwed.

Provide your vendors with as much helpful information as you can. This might mean swatches of the fabric of the bridesmaid dresses for the florist so she can find matching ribbon. It might mean a list of all the VIPs so your photographer can be sure to capture them all on film (or pixels). Make sure you ask all the questions you have about the pro's service. It could be anything from what their packages include to what they'll wear on the wedding day.

You should meet with three vendors, because with three, you'll get a good idea of different styles, attitudes, and personalities. Any fewer, and you might be limiting yourself. That said, if you see three vendors and aren't impressed or don't make a connection, you'll need to see more. Trust your instincts.

Once you find a vendor who meets your approval, it's time to crack open that checkbook. To secure their services, it's customary to leave a deposit. Although the exact amount and percentage will vary, never, and I mean never, pay in full before the service is completed. If a vendor asks or insists on this, walk out of there. When it comes to price, feel free to negotiate, especially if there are services offered in the packages that you don't want. Ask what you can save by cutting some features. You might even have two different vendors give you a quote, then see if the more expensive guy will match the lower offer—this isn't a common practice, but since it works with plumbers, it might also work with wedding vendors. Then, get everything in writing to the smallest detail. If you despise daffodils and don't want even one yellow petal at your wedding, or refuse to have strawberries on your cake because they'll make your tongue swell up like an inflatable raft, be sure that those demands are written in your contract.

> "My groom and I worked with our florist to design a floral arrangement in memory of our departed relatives with subdued white flowers. When my now-husband got to the site on our wedding day, he saw arrangements made of bright pink carnations! And the floral designer told him, 'Go get a broom and sweep up these petals and leaves we dropped.' The nerve!"
>
> —Stephanie

In the end, you want to give your vendors as much information about your wedding as possible—and *get* as much information as you can from them, both verbally and in writing, about the services they're going to be performing for you, so you might actually get some shuteye this year.

START SPREADING THE NEWS

Unless you want to use Evite to get the word out to your guests, you're going to have to send paper invitations. Since this invitation will be the first glimpse into the festivities, it should set the theme, tone, and individuality of your wedding day. Personally, I regret choosing my boring invitations. Not only did I get two other identical wedding invites later that year, but the invitations gave the impression that we would be dining on oatmeal and milk toast at our reception.

If you have plenty of time before your wedding day, or if you have guests that will need to travel to the event, or if your wedding will be on a busy holiday weekend, or, hell, if you just like them, you can also send a save-the-date card before the proper invitation. These cards get the word out in advance of the invitations to avoid any scheduling conflicts. However, if you don't send one, no one will miss it, so it's a good place to save some cash.

A save-the-date should hit guests' mailboxes about four months before the wedding (the invites will then follow two months later), but you can send yours even further in advance if you think guests need extra time to make travel plans. You don't need a lot of detail on your save the date, but be sure to include the who, what, when, and a *general* where. In other words, give people a preview. You want them to know that your wedding is taking place in Boston on the Saturday of Memorial Day weekend. If they *probably* don't need to book their reservations in advance, that's all you really need. But if they'll need to book a long time ahead, you might want to include the actual venue or resort information so that they can make the appropriate plans. I once got a save-the-date that had the couple's names and the date on it, but there was no city listed! If it's not evident, include the city.

Unlike the formal invitation, you can get pretty inventive and creative with a save-the-date card. I recently saw one where "Save the Date . . . or we wrote on his head for nothing!" was written on the groom's bald head in marker. The wide-eyed bride was pointing and smiling. It showed that this couple had a pretty cool sense of humor and most likely got plenty of guests' attention. Another couple—huge Bruce Springsteen fans—had their picture taken in the style of Bruce on the *Born in the USA* album cover for their save the dates. They even wrote "Born to wed!" at the bottom. I've seen so many other save-the-date ideas, from postcards to magnets to some that were shaped like plane tickets, or included a homemade cookie or DVD. The sky's the limit!

The invitation, on the other hand, should be a little less casual. I won't bore you with the different printing styles and invitation "looks." You can find that info at sites like TheKnot.com and Brides.com. You can also look through different styles and looks that fit your event. In the back of the book, you will find a list of some of my favorite stationery designers—check out their sites.

Incorporating aspects of your wedding in your invitation design is a nice touch. Say you're decorating with blue hydrangeas—can you find an invite with hydrangeas on them? A pretty starfish design for a beach wedding? Remember that yes, a formal wedding invite should be very simple, but that doesn't mean you can't get creative with fonts, borders, ink colors, and even the envelope liners. Avoid cartoon brides and grooms and photos of the two of you—photo cards definitely work for a save-the-date but they're kinda cheesy for an invitation (unless it's a super-casual wedding).

Invitation Regulation

Invitations can be the biggest thorn in the wedding planning bouquet. If you don't follow the rules, you can be stuck having to reorder them and then not be able to get them out in time. To prevent this, here are some basic guidelines to follow:

Etiquette states that wedding invitations should be mailed six to eight weeks before the event. However, in order for that to happen, you have to order and proof them with enough time for them to arrive, get the envelopes addressed (some people do this professionally, which adds even more time), add postage for the reply cards and adornments, and get them in the mail. Plus, before you step foot in the stationery store to pick out invitations, you need to have your caterer squared away because your RSVP cards might need to include your guests' meal preference. I once interviewed a bride who said her biggest mistake was going into a stationery shop to order her wedding invitations and then realizing she didn't know all the pertinent information for her event. She had to scramble to call her wedding venue and figure out the right time for the ceremony to start. That's not something you want to decide in a pinch. And you don't want to be stuck having to reorder invitations that have mistakes on them—that will cost *mucho dinero.*

You should also have a firm invitee list planned before you pick out invitations. Remember, you don't need to order one invitation per guest, but rather, one invitation per family household. If you have friends who are roommates (and not a couple), however, they should each get their own invite. Once you have a firm number of invitations, and all the pertinent info to put on them, you're good to go.

When ordering invitations, it's crucial to order a few extras. I can't tell you how many brides make mistakes addressing envelopes and don't have any leftover. A few more invites are also handy for last minute friends you want to include, people who said they never received an invitation (or more likely lost theirs), or new clients of your dad that you're now being forced to invite because he's paying for the wedding and won't let you forget it.

When you're at the stationery store, ask the pros to help you with the wording of your invite. The way you phrase the details can really help set the tone. Check out some sample ways to phrase invitations at their store or at VerseIt.com. Once the proof of your invitation is done, make sure you double-check for misspellings, typos, wrong information, etc.—even people who copyedit manuscripts for a living still don't always find all the mistakes! That's why it's a good idea to have at least two other people proofread the invite. Make sure you've covered the who, what, when, and where completely and that everyone's name is spelled correctly.

While you're ordering, think ahead to the wedding and the other paper products you might need. Would you like matching menu cards, escort cards, table numbers, and thank you notes? It's not necessary for all this stuff to match, but sometimes you can get a deal when you order it all together. Plus, some brides really love having a theme that ties together all the wedding stationery.

Once you have your invitations in hand, you have to address the envelopes. Etiquette nazis dictate you need to have these hand lettered by a calligrapher, but this is expensive and

time consuming! You can learn how to do calligraphy yourself, but it will be a slow road if you have a lot of guests (not
to mention painful, because you'll have to hold your bouquet
with carpal tunnel syndrome). It's fine to write them neatly by
hand with a nice pen. No, people, this does not mean a Bic.
Alternatively, you can also address invites the more modern
way: with your computer. Even non–technologically savvy
people know how to "mail merge." This means taking an
Excel spreadsheet full of addresses and making it into labels
or printing them directly onto the envelopes. Choose a nice
script-like font, ideally the same one on the invitation itself.
If you need to do this on labels, select clear ones that will
blend in with the envelope. Because even though you counting RSVPs will be a little bit like counting chads, you're running a wedding, not a political campaign.

Another potential problem is not allowing for enough
time to stuff envelopes because you don't realize how long it
will take. To save time, and your sanity, don't do this alone!
Invite your bridesmaids, mom, aunts, friends—whomever
you want—to your home for a little vino and envelope stuffing party. If you have a lot of invites, a lot of friends, and
definitely a lot of wine, it could make for a very fun party
indeed.

And finally, a huge mistake soon-to-be brides make
is to simply go to the post office for stamps, stick them
on, and put the invites in the mailbox. Rookie mistake!
What's missing from this plan is the new freakin' rules and
measures for postage. If your invite is square or another
non-rectangular shape, is *smaller* than 3½ by 5 by .007
inches, is *larger* than 6⅛ by 11½ by ¼ inches, or weighs
more than 3.5 ounces, it will cost more to send it than the
standard postage rate for letters (postage can easily cost

more than the invitation!). Also, if you've got a ribbon or anything else that will make the invitation bumpy— called "nonmachinable" by the lovely post office—it can also up the postage. The solution is to assemble one entire invitation, with all the enclosures, accessories, seals, and whatnot and bring it by hand to the post office of your choice. Have the staff weigh it and tell you how much it will cost to mail it. Otherwise, you're really taking a gamble. I can't tell you how many brides I know who got all their beautiful invites returned with an ugly stamp that read "postage due." Ugh!

As you can see, sending out your wedding invitations in time, and without mistakes, is a big challenge. But if you heed these warnings, and have some good friends to help, you'll be rewarded by a steady stream of RSVP cards in your mailbox!

How to Save on Invitations

Don't have a lot of cash for professional invitations? Make your own. There's a vast selection of lovely papers designed to fit in your printer that you can customize yourself. Retail outlets such as Target often have beautiful DIY invites. If you decide to go this route, proceed with caution.

TEN QUESTIONS TO ASK BEFORE YOU DIY

1. Do I have a good quality printer and does my computer have plenty of stylish fonts to choose from?
2. How do I do with craft projects normally—am I prone to screwing them up?
3. How much time do I have to devote to this project?
4. Do I need a professional's help deciding on the right words to use?

5. Do I follow directions well?
6. Do I have plenty of space in my home for all the supplies needed for this project?
7. Is the amount of money I'll save worth the amount of time I'll spend doing this?
8. Do I have someone to help me?
9. Do I have my heart set on a professional printing style, i.e., raised or letterpress printing?
10. Have I ordered extra supplies in case of errors or ink smears?

Sure, wedding invites can be a little annoying and stuffy, what with all those rules and etiquette and formality and stuff. Plus, there's more you want to say to guests, right? Here's where the wedding website comes in.

Webbing Invitation

Many couples create wedding websites to notify their guests about details of the wedding that don't fit on the invitation or save the date. This is especially nice to do if a lot of out-of-towners are attending or if it's a destination wedding. Of course, it's also one more thing to add to your mounting to-do list, and hiring a web designer to create something worthy of a Webby award is quite tempting.

But be realistic here. Your wedding website should simply be a go-to place where guests can find hotel information and in-town restaurant recommendations. Their visits to your wedding website will most likely be short and will happen when they need to remember what time the ceremony starts so they can pick the best flight, or where you registered when they want to get you a gift. So keep it simple and affordable.

There are plenty of services that let you create a wedding website for free: TheKnot.com, WeddingChannel.com, and eWedding.com are just a few. But remember that it doesn't *have* to be a *wedding* website provider. You could simply set up your own site and go from there—Webs.com offers free no-frills websites. Usually, it just costs a small fee if you want some extra features and if you want a special URL, like "tinaanddaveswedding.com" or something of the sort.

Luckily, if you can use word processing software, e-mail, and Facebook, it's not difficult to figure out how to create the site. (Hell, if you want, you can just set up a Facebook page for your wedding and call it a day.) Usually the providers offer templates that make it easy to fill in the pertinent details about the wedding day and insert a cute photo of you and your fiancé where applicable. If you're stumped, there are often tutorials as well.

Set up your wedding website as early as you can and fill in details of the wedding as you plan them. To spread the word, either e-mail everyone you can with a link to the site, include the URL on your save the date, or include a very tasteful card in your invitation envelope with the URL. Consider setting the site up to be password-protected and pass the secret code on to your family and friends. There is the unlikely possibility that a burglar will see the site and in turn know exactly when you and all of your next of kin definitely *won't* be home.

Your website should definitely include:

- Your and your groom's names
- The wedding date and any times you know
- The locations and their addresses

- Hotel information
- Where you're registered

You might want to also consider adding:

- Suggestions of things for guests to do while they're in town.
- Details about pre- and after-parties like the rehearsal dinner and next day brunch—but only if everyone is invited.
- Some information about what type of event to expect and the formality of dress. This is especially important if, for example, you're having an Indian wedding and you want to encourage guests to wear cultural garb, or you're having a casual celebration where Uncle John donning his 30-year-old tuxedo would not be appropriate.
- Simple links to hotels, restaurants, and attractions' websites—or their phone number and address—usually provide enough information for guests looking to make a weekend out of the wedding. If there's a place or tradition that's especially meaningful to you two, you can describe the sentimental reasons behind choosing it.

If you really want to go crazy, you can also include:

- The names of the wedding party and other VIPs
- A photo album of you and the groom
- A description of how you met

Considering that most guests do not have all day to scroll through the photos from your vacation to Bermuda, you probably want to skip a lot of these extras for the sake of your own time and sanity. You also don't want to look completely self-absorbed by writing a novel about yourself and posting it on the Net.

FOOD FOR THOUGHT

Sure, a wedding is a time for two people in love to start their lives together, but more importantly, it's a time to chow down on some incredible food. However, sometimes wedding food is barely one step above airline food. One of the factors that contributes to this is that many couples feel they need to serve crowd pleasers and that translates to "traditional" wedding fare. Read: boring. Usually it's the choice of a blah steak and blaher chicken or salmon or tilapia or some other non–red-meat-stuff. Stick it on a plate with a side of overcooked broccoli and mashed potatoes that look like they came out of a Reddi-wip can, and you've got yourself a wedding menu!

Then there are the people who think they can please all the people all the time by serving "duos" (i.e., surf 'n' turf), but all these dishes do is leave all of the people hungry. If someone likes surf, they want a nice plate of surf, not half a serving of surf and an equally small serving of turf which they didn't want in the first place. The only winner of the duo concept is the waitstaff who get to sneak back in the kitchen and scarf down all the untouched food.

So, I urge you, when it comes to planning the wedding menu, think outside the cardboard flavored food box. Need inspiration? Think of your and your fiancé's favorite foods. Or perhaps foods that are symbolic in your lives. Maybe you got engaged in South Africa and can serve African food. Perhaps you can get inspiration from your heritage. Indian food is great if that's what your family is used to and loves—plus, it will show guests how important your culture is to you. Or maybe your heritage will help you decide what not to serve. I'm half Italian-American, and I wouldn't dare serve something like ravioli or manicotti at my wedding because my Italian family members would consider it a complete and utter sin unless it came from my grandmother's kitchen!

What if your fiancé's family is Chinese and expects authentic Chinese food at a wedding and your family doesn't eat anything but meat and potatoes? The last thing you want is a food fight at your wedding! That's where the whole creative thing comes into play. Maybe you have Asian hors d'oeuvres during the cocktail hour and a more American wedding menu for the dinner. Or maybe you can find Chinese foods to serve for dinner that even the unadventurous eaters can appreciate. Listen, you're never going to make everyone happy with the food. But make yourselves happy, and a few wedding guest VIPs like your parents and future in-laws, and you've got a good meal plan.

Once you've got your wedding menu locked down, you'll need to find a caterer to pull it off. Look for one that specializes in your choice of cuisine. Of course, you might not have much of a choice if your venue comes with its own kitchen staff, in which case forget everything I just said and choose from a designated menu. Even then, maybe they can be flexible . . . a few dashes of hot sauce turns regular chicken into chicken that's mucho caliente!

Now comes my favorite part: the tasting! You and your fiancé get to dig in and sample all the goodies your caterer whips up for you. It's like having your own personal chef! Come hungry and savor every bite. There are no rules here, only suggestions.

- If you and your mate have any changes for a certain dish, be sure you try it before you finalize your decision. It's best not to serve anything at your wedding that you haven't tasted yourself.
- Unless you have a kickback deal in place with the local dry cleaners, drippy finger food is out.
- When it comes to serving the food, buffet-style is a good choice so guests can pick and choose what they want to eat from an array of selections. If you don't want guests to have to stand in line cafeteria style, consider having platters of food served family style on each table or offer two or more specific entrée choices.
- Think about your guests. Do you have a lot of vegetarian, kosher, or vegan guests or guests with food allergies? If there are only a few, you can let your caterer know who they are so they can whip something up for them accordingly, but if there are a lot on your guest list, one of your main entrée choices should reflect that preference (I wouldn't worry so much about approving that dish beforehand unless you're a fan of bean curd mash or chickpea surprise).
- Once you select your menu and start drawing up your contract, ask your caterer to pack up some wedding meal leftovers on the day of the event and have it sent to your hotel room or getaway car. That way, no matter how much craziness happens that day, you get the chance to enjoy it. Because after the dilemma of choosing the perfect meal and plopping down the

big check to pay for it, most brides and grooms are so busy greeting guests and posing for photos, they're lucky to eat one bite.

ANNIE LEIBOVITZ, GLAMOUR SHOTS, OR SOMEWHERE IN BETWEEN

Unlike the other things you painstakingly plan for your wedding day, there are few you'll get to keep after it's over: an invitation, the dress, and of course, any photographic and videographic evidence that your wedding even took place. Considering this, you don't want to leave the photos up to Grampa Pat who graciously offered his services despite his shaky hands and glaucoma.

Yes, professional photographers are pricey, and it's tempting to go with whoever's the cheapest, but, with few exceptions, you really do get what you pay for. I have friends who made this mistake and ended up with photos that were so bad, they ended up not buying any. If you're on a tight budget, I recommend nixing the professional video and concentrating solely on some good quality photography, instead of going with a crappy photographer and a crappy videographer. I know tons of people who look through their wedding pictures often or display some favorite shots from the big day around their home, but there aren't too many who sit down to a half hour long video on a regular basis. It's just not realistic.

If you are planning to have both, pick a photog you love first. Then ask that pro for videographer recommendations. The photographer will probably be able to point out some people he's worked with before whose style he likes and who he works well with. Remember, sometimes the photographer and videographer are standing side-by-side, competing for the best shots, and you don't want any *Jersey Shore*–type smack downs.

There are several different photography styles out there. Some are more traditional and take lots of posed pictures. Others are documentary style and capture in-the-moment candids. Some use photographic techniques to "enhance" the images. Many do a combination of at least two of these styles. Honestly, you don't need to know anything about photography in order to choose a good photographer. You just need to look at the pros' previous work to get a feel for what they do. Don't be fooled by pictures of expensive look-ing weddings! Look at the pictures themselves, not the fabu-lous flowers in the background. Ask to see an album of *one* complete wedding, not just a "greatest hits" from a bunch of different ones. That way, you can get a sense of the pho-tographer's consistency and what he can do for you for your event. When it comes right down to it, the most important thing is that you get someone who takes good photos and who's reliable.

There are often several ways to go when it comes to price. You can buy the photos individually, or many pho-tographers offer package deals that include the album. This is because they make a nice profit from the sale of an album. If money is an issue, try to find a photographer that's willing to sell you a CD of your photos so you can order your own pictures. Not everyone will do this because it's not always economical. If you go this route, make sure the CD is hi-resolution so the prints will be professional quality instead of something that looks like it was taken with a cell phone.

After all that information, you might be wondering whether or not you should get the video. Like everything else, it's up to you (and that fiancé of yours). There are some really lovely wedding videos. And if you don't want a long one that rivals the running time of *Avatar*, ask a videographer to make you a five-minute film. They can even give you a video file that you can upload on your iPod or Facebook. It's pretty sweet. Videos can also capture things that photos can't, like your laughter when you flub up your vows, or that really cute toast your dad makes.

"We interviewed a photographer who lived in a filthy, smelly trailer. We were hesitant from the start, but asked to see wedding albums of his work. He handed us books filled with pictures of women in bikinis holding different kinds of snakes. We hightailed it out of there as fast as possible."

—Melissa

Don't be discouraged by videographers if your only experience with them was at your cousin's bar mitzvah in 1996. Technology has come a long way and now pros can shoot with BluRay and HD quality. Also, videographers don't need to lug around giant camcorders and stadium lights they way they used to. The most bothersome thing about being videotaped might be a tiny, cordless mic your groom has to pin to his lapel during the ceremony. That's it. And in the end, you're left with a wonderful souvenir that you can savor, or accidentally tape over, in the years to follow.

UN-EASY LISTENING

Unless you want to entertain your guests by enticing them into a round of "Row, Row, Row Your Boat," you're going to have to hire a band or DJ. There are pros and cons with each, but since nine out of ten brides hire a DJ, let's start with them.

A DJ is a really smart buy—cheap, simple, and straightforward. And unlike a band, a DJ can play any song you can dream of as long as they sell it on iTunes.

A good, experienced DJ will be able to take requests from the crowd, observe guests' moods and reactions to certain types of songs, and make choices accordingly.

The main downfall of a DJ is that some people think they're cheesy. Many aren't even music experts but rather people who want to earn a few bucks on the weekend and love to talk. And man, can some of them talk! It's like they think your wedding is the Super Bowl and it needs constant commentary. If this is a concern, let them know in advance what you expect. Tell them you don't need someone to chant, "Go Aunt Tina, go Aunt Tina" over and over on a PA system. When our DJ explained that the dancing at a wedding starts off with the bride leading the Chicken Dance, we said, "Under no circumstances do we want the Chicken Dance, the Hokey Pokey, the Macarena, or any other line dance song played." We told him we'd prefer less talking and more music and were specific about the music we did want. He acted like we were crazy, but said he'd go along. I was worried it all went in one ear and out the other, but during the reception, one of my cousins came to me, dejected, because the DJ wouldn't meet her request for The Electric Slide, and I smiled ear to ear. We talked and he listened.

Success! Most DJs will totally respect any "Do Not Play" or "Must Play" list you provide, so feel free to do so.

> "Right when I was about to walk down the aisle, a fire siren blasted down the street of the church, so my dad told me to wait. When it stopped, I noticed that the organ music sounded just horrible. Turns out the original organist never showed up, and her nephew filled in. It would have sounded better if I walked down the aisle to the fire siren."
>
> —Sandi

In the world of realistic budgets, bands really do play second fiddle to DJs. In fact, in the past few years, I've only attended one wedding that used a band, but it kicked ass. Bands might have their drawbacks, but there's nothing better than the personal, interactive quality they provide. They feed off the energy of the crowd and guests feed off of them in return. There's something slick about having a band at your reception. But with every high note comes a low one, such as the hefty prices bands tend to charge. They also have limited playlists. A band has more members, meaning more people to pay and feed. They also have more equipment, so you'll need plenty of space in your reception room for the band. You also need to find a way to fill in the time while the band takes breaks. Some brides have a DJ play or select a few prerecorded songs for these time periods.

There is a third option that's geared for the budget conscious wedding: the self-DJ'ed iPod wedding. This strategy will save you serious cash, and you and your intended can have complete control over the playlist. The main drawback is no one at your wedding can make a request (although is that really a bad thing?) and, if you're not technologically savvy, you run the risk of suddenly hearing Chapter 7 of *The DaVinci Code* audiobook play after your first dance. If you go the self DJ'ed iPod route, be sure to check, and recheck, your final playlist!

FLOWERS: THE POWER TO MAKE YOU HAVE A NERVOUS BREAKDOWN

You'd think ordering flowers would be the no-brainer of the wedding planning world. You simply prance in the store, sit with the florist, and tell her what you want. The flowers arrive on your wedding day looking fresh and fantastic and your guests rave for years to come. Unfortunately, this scenario is far from the truth. In real life, the flowers can arrive wilted, and in different colors and varieties than you agreed upon. Yup, there's nothing as frustrating as spending a blooming fortune on blooms that are less than you'd expect.

For my wedding, the florist delivered bridesmaid bouquets that were much smaller than we agreed upon. And she brought the flower girl a basket full of pink petals—even though the rest of my flowers were white and blue—and bragged to my mother that I would *love* it. I did not.

Even when I was working on big budget NY photo shoots for a bridal magazine, I still had problems with the flowers. I'd ask florists to make arrangements and bouquets to certain specifications and, no matter how much I discussed the plan, I never knew what was going to show up on the day of the photo shoot. Unfortunately, that's what a lot of brides experience, and wedding days cannot be reshot.

However, there are things you can do to stack the odds in your favor. For one, use a florist that comes highly recommended (I can't stress the importance of personal recommendations enough). Also, bring in photos of arrangements you like, as well as swatches of the bridesmaids gowns. Give your florist a list of your flower favorites, and the varieties that you want nothing to do with. If possible, have the florist create a sample bouquet and centerpiece. That way you can both look at a finished product and make tweaks from there. A single bouquet can be quite expensive, so some florists might protest—but being unhappy with your flowers could be more costly. I mean, doesn't she want you to recommend her services to your family and friends?

Anyone who's bought flowers before knows they can be expensive. Your bridal bouquet alone could cost $100 to $200. Add bridesmaids' bouquets, centerpieces, boutonnieres, corsages, and a flower girl basket, and you're talking some serious dough. One money saving trick is to choose flowers that are in-season. These will be the most affordable, the longest lasting, and the easiest to get. The last thing you want to do is rely on spring lilacs that have to be flown in from South America in the middle of winter. Sit down with your florist and say, "Here are my colors. Here's the style I like. You pick the freshest, most beautiful flowers for the best price." Another trick to save money is to purchase your own vases and vessels, since some floral designers select pricey things or tack on quite the upcharge. Michael's, AC Moore, and other craft shops are bound to have some good affordable options. One wedding planner I worked with on a photo shoot liked to get them from Ikea where vases are mad cheap. You can also save money by adding fruit to your centerpieces along with the flowers.

"My husband is in the Air Force, so we cut our cake with a sword. When we finished cutting our bites, he turned to me and said, 'How many pieces do I have to cut?' He thought he had to cut slices for all 150 guests. To this day, he is adamant that he was only kidding but I'm not so sure."

—Melanie

In the end, flowers are unpredictable and can stress you out, but the more flexible you are with them, the more money you'll save. Chances are, the flowers will be a huge headache yet turn out lovely. And if they don't, well . . . honestly, have you ever heard anyone say, "I would have had so much fun at that wedding if only the flowers had been prettier?" Me neither.

SO MUCH FOR A CAKE WALK

For something so sweet, wedding cakes can be pretty frigging aggravating. Planning the cake sounds like nothing but fun and games. You meet the baker, you taste a bunch of delicious flavor combos (I recommend at least three cake flavors and three filling flavors), your pro gets creative and whips up something 100 percent original and gorgeous and then, *voilà*, you have one masterful confection worthy of so many oohs and aaahs that it should be forbidden to cut into it, and instead, it should be bronzed to last a lifetime. But in reality the cake isn't quite so easy and breezy. Here's why:

The Cake Boss makes it look easy, but it's actually infinitely tough to find a baker who excels at baking a cake that both tastes good and looks beautiful. Too many brides focus on the *style* of the wedding and don't really care whether or not the cake that's served tastes like paste. Call me a skeptic, but what's the point of a cake that no one wants to eat? Make sure you taste and taste well before you book your baker.

Many wedding cake bakers will have you look through their books and pick a cake that you like, then make it for you in your wedding colors. That's totally fine if you don't care about originality, but if you want something unique or that doesn't fit in your pro's wheelhouse, you're going to have to put a lot of trust in this baker to pull it off. Ask for a sketch from your cake pro and make sure you approve of it long before the big day.

Many bakers work with the florist to get fresh flowers to put on the cake. This involves communication between the two vendors, so if you want fresh flowers on your cake, consider hiring a florist he's worked with often—or vice versa.

Wedding cakes are packed in cardboard boxes and hauled to ceremony sites in the back of trucks or vans. Yes, as long as the baker you hired is experienced, he has probably transported hundreds of cakes this way and has it down pat. That does not mean a fender bender or massive pothole couldn't ruin your cake. Unfortunately, there's nothing you can do but pray to the dessert gods and hope your baker carries an extra tube of frosting along on deliveries.

There are also some traditions involved with cakes that could be interpreted by some as silly or sentimental. Here's what to consider when deciding whether or not to partake:

The Cake Cutting—and Mashing

When it comes to the obligatory cake cutting, there are two schools of thought. One, to elegantly feed each other a forkful of cake while looking lovingly into each other's eyes. The other, to go hog wild *à la* the food fight scene in *Animal House*. Now, I firmly believe that if you want to let loose and have a bit of a cake fight fun with the groom, go right ahead. But you two need to be in agreement on this before hand. Thirty-five years later, my mom is *still* mad at my dad for smashing cake in her face. Also, avoid colored frosting and flavors such as black forest or red velvet, which have the potential to stain your dress and veil.

Top Tier Saving—and Freezing

I can't decide whether the idea of saving the top tier of the wedding cake and eating it on your first anniversary is nicely sentimental, or if it's just a ploy made up by cake bakers to get you to buy more cake. My husband and I did this, not just because we're sentimental and perhaps a bit superstitious, but because hey, we like cake! After a year in our freezer, the cake was surprisingly good, but the frosting had completely changed consistency and was pretty much inedible. If you're grossed out by freezer burn, consider bypassing this tradition. You can either ask the baker to do without an extra tier, or if you like tall cakes, consider taking it back to the hotel suite with you and eating it off each other's naked bodies on the wedding night.

Now you've got your vendors and your contracts. You even have a list of their phone numbers and email addresses in case of a big day emergency. Deposits are paid and final payments are in their specially labeled envelopes ready for the best man to hand to each vendor when they deliver the goods on the wedding day. Does this guarantee a lemon cake won't show up when you requested coconut? Does it mean that your DJ won't try to slip in a little bit of Master P during the reception? Or that the hotel's air conditioning won't zonk out during your August bash? Sorry, but I can't promise any of this to you. At least these tips will give you enough peace of mind to be able to enjoy the wedding day without gnawing off your French manicure before the ring's even on your finger.

Chapter 7

"Shower" Refers to Your Gifts, Not Your Tears

As soon as your man gets up from bended knee, it sets off an onslaught of parties, lunches, gatherings, and bachelorette shindigs. As if planning a wedding isn't exhausting enough! Fortunately, these parties aren't your responsibility to plan. And *unfortunately*, these parties aren't your responsibility to plan. Even though your friends and family may take on the brunt of the work, you'll be paying the price as well.

If you like being in control, you're basically screwed because you'll have to hand off the party planning reins to someone else (and may hate the results). You may feel judged if the party is boring or the food is unpalatable, even though you didn't lift a finger. There may be hurt feelings, and you'll have to tend to complaints from friends or family who were innocently omitted from the guest list. You may feel guilty because of the large sums of money your hosts need to spend in order to throw you a shower, or the amount your guests need to spring on multitude gifts.

You naively believe the only thing you need to do for your parties is put on a pretty dress and *ooh* and *ahhh* at all your great gifts. And while there will be a pretty dress involved, and, if you've registered right, plenty of great gifts, there will also be some headaches too. These parties are not all fun and games (oh yeah, I haven't even mentioned those corny shower games!), but perhaps, with a little preparation, you can lessen the suck factor.

THE ENGAGEMENT PARTY

The first celebration on the party circuit is the appropriately titled "engagement party." Engagement parties aren't as common as some of the other pre-wedding bashes. In fact, I've never been to an actual engagement party but, like men who enjoy vacuuming and babies that are born sleeping through the night, I'm told they do exist. The reason for this party is to celebrate the fact that after all the dating, the breakups, the makeup sex, the getting back together, the moving in, the moving out, the moving back in . . . the two of you are finally getting hitched! What a perfect opportunity to gather your closest friends and family around, have a toast, and show off your gorgeous rock. But like your sheets after that makeup sex, things can get rather sticky!

To begin with, you have to find someone to throw you this party. Emily Post would frown upon throwing it yourself. Sure, if you don't give a crap about Emily, go ahead and do it . . . just don't expect Emily to show up. If no one offers to host you the party, you can drop a few hints, but your hands are basically tied. This doesn't mean your friends are losers or that they hate your fiancé and think you should drop kick him back in the dating pool. It may just mean that these people are busy with their lives or they've been to enough weddings to know how expensive they are. There will be shower gifts, wedding presents, clothing expenses, and possibly even airline tickets and hotel rooms to buy. Hosting an engagement party may be a good place to cut back.

If you're lucky and have a friend or family member offer to throw you a party, your main, and only, responsibility will be to provide your host with a guest list. But remember, think small. At this early point in the game, you don't have your guest list locked down for your wedding yet and you'd hate to make the faux pas of inviting someone to the engagement party that you don't end up inviting to the wedding. This will really piss Emily off! My best advice is to invite only close family and friends. You might want to omit out-of-towners, extended family, and co-workers, but proceed with caution. You want anyone who's not invited to the bash to know that it was just a small event so you don't risk hurting anyone's feelings if they hear there was a party and they weren't privy.

If you're lucky, your hosts may ask for some guidance in what kind of party to throw. But, if you're not (and you're usually not), they will plan the whole thing without your input. If they plan a casual daytime picnic when you had your heart set on an evening cocktail party, it's best to suck it up, put on some bug spray, and head to the park. If nothing's been planned yet, you can certainly, very politely, state your wishes, but if things are already underway, it's best to leave it be. The last thing you want to do is upset someone who could end up being your bridesmaid. The only exception is if their party will create a serious problem. For example, if your friends tell you they're planning a rooftop affair and you have a dreadful fear of heights and will spend the whole time with heart palpitations and sweaty palms, speak

Planning Your Wedding Sucks

up. Shy of that, let them do their thing. Bask in the moment and the people you love who are there to celebrate with you.

In general, engagement parties are pretty low key, so don't expect a bunch of pomp and circumstance, or grand gifts (most people will bring small ones, similar to a hostess gift, like a bottle of wine or a punch bowl. Some won't give gifts at all, and that's Kosher too). Just an intimate gathering of family and friends with some food and drink, engagement parties are pretty much the coolest and most relaxed part of the pre-wedding parties, so enjoy it while it lasts.

PICKING THE BRIDAL PARTY: MORE IMPORTANT THAN PICKING YOUR GROOM (KIDDING. SORT OF.)

After the big *woo hoo!* of the engagement party comes the first of many decisions: who to ask to be in your bridal party. If you decide to have a traditional bridal party, choose the bridesmaids and groomsmen early—not only to help with dress shopping and tux renting decisions but also because these people will be VIPs at all the pre-wedding events.

Whether you're having a small ceremony or large, you'll most likely want some special people by your side. Bridesmaids. Groomsmen. A best man. A maid of honor. There's something nice about bringing together our best friends from different phases of our lives and have them stand by our side for a day—or for several days if you include the shower, bachelorette party, and rehearsal dinner too. The suck factor includes hurting the feelings of people you don't ask, people who say "yes" but really just don't give a shit about doing things for your wedding, and finding out after the wedding day that said bridal party member is a jerk—and there they are in all the wedding photos for you to "treasure." So how exactly do you decide whom to put through the torture of pastel dresses and paintball bachelor parties with your degenerate teenage cousins? As with all parties, the first thing to consider is the guest list.

If your wedding guest list is exclusive, the wedding party is like getting into MENSA. Only invite people that you can imagine being in your life fifty years from now. Think about those gal-pals who can survive the stresses of your wedding and still love you after dealing with your constant inflamed emotions for the next year or so. Siblings and dear cousins are always fair game—and may actually be peeved if they don't make the short list. Then there are those tried-and-true friends who've stuck by you through bad haircuts and bad breakups. Avoid asking your new friend at work that started having lunch with you but may dump your ass if she gets promoted. This is to avoid previously mentioned burnable photos.

While you choose a wedding party, remember that anything goes these days. Your male best friend can stand by *your* side as Man of Honor, and your fiancé's sister can be a groomswoman. I only caution against choosing anyone your future husband doesn't like or anyone either of you has slept with. Besides that, the rules about wedding parties are so flexible today that you can dress your dogs in tuxes and have them be ringbearers, so don't let antiquated rules govern your decisions. (Beware that Great Aunt Lenore will probably think that having your male best friend on the girls' side is horrific, but who gives a poot what Great Aunt Lenore thinks?) If you do, however, dream of the typical, gender-divided wedding party, you might have to give in and let his sister be your bridesmaid. You can suggest that your male bestie be a groomsman, but your guy doesn't have to oblige.

When it comes to choosing your maid of honor, choose wisely. It's a big job and like all jobs, you need to pick someone qualified. Before they agree, warn them of everything you'll request them to do. Tell her she's going to have to head up the bridal shower planning, corral the girls' dress measurements and deposit money, and pack up a wedding-day emergency kit. Ask her if she feels comfortable organizing this stuff and occasionally having to be the one barking orders or asking for money. If she doesn't, avoid bitching her out, as much as you really want to. It can be hurtful to hear that someone doesn't want to go out of their way to be your maid of honor, but let it go and try not to let it get in the way of your friendship. Besides, you have more important things to worry about. Instead, choose someone else who relishes the leadership position. But if you really want your irresponsible, shy, or impossible-to-get-along-with sister to be your maid of honor, and she's willing to do it, it may be best to ask a married friend to be the "matron of honor" as well, and she can share duties with Sis.

While some of us dread being bridesmaids, there are those rare friends who are offended because they weren't asked to be in the wedding party. You're liable to get reamed out, ignored, or receive some other passive-aggressive treatment from a friend like that. If there's someone close to you who you think might be one of those friends, head off any hissy fits by nicely explaining to her that you wanted to ask her but you just have too many sisters or that your guy didn't have enough groomsmen candidates and you wanted the same number of girls and guys. Ask her if she'd be willing to participate in the big day in another way, such as giving a meaningful reading at the ceremony, greeting and seating guests, or just teaming up with you on shopping trips and pre-wedding pedicures.

There are also those people who you don't necessarily want to be bridesmaids but you have no choice but to choose, like your bratty fourteen-year-old cousin and your evil step-sister. You might not have much say in asking these people to be in the wedding party, unless of course, you decide to have an *extremely* small wedding party and by that I mean one maid of honor and one best man and that's it. Yep. Do that.

How to Avoid Bridal Party Poopers

Once you've made your wedding party choice, take a look at who's coming together for this event—it might be a sort of motley crew. A work friend, an old college roomie, your second cousin—these people might be wonderful and amazing friends to you. But that doesn't necessarily mean they'll be friends to each other. It doesn't even mean they'll get along *at all*. And while it seems like it will be a ton of fun having girl bonding events like a bridesmaid spa day and a pre-shower decorating party, it is very likely that things will be awkward or tenuous.

Let go of the idea that this should be easy—or that you have no responsibility for helping these women perform their bridesmaids' duties or for helping them enjoy themselves while they're doing them. Make it your responsibility to break the ice between them. A gathering beforehand that includes a lot of wine could definitely help. But what you really want to do is open the lines of communication. Supply the ladies with each others' e-mail addresses and phone numbers. "Suggest" they become Facebook friends. (But don't expect them to become BFFs—or get jealous if they *do*.) Call each one

and tell them—nicely, of course—exactly what you expect of
them as bridesmaids. Let them know you'll appreciate all the
hard work and the time and money they'll be spending along
the way. Of course, clarifying friendship, asking for favors,
and discussing money are on no one's list of favorite activi-
ties. So I can see how you may dread this conversation. This
can be a sticky situation for you as the bride and for them as
potential bridesmaids. Many people feel they just don't have
the resources or time for all that party planning and money-
shelling-out. And let's face it, when people are posed with
a scenario that they don't expect—like committing at least
three Saturdays this year to your wedding—they don't always
react well. You might experience a potential bridesmaid who
responds with a one-word answer, who asks you a million
questions, or who completely freaks out at the mere mention
of bridesmaid-dom. So even if you're looking forward to this
conversation, be sure to tread lightly:

Make it a question, not an order. You don't want anyone to feel cornered into being your bridesmaid, so make
sure she knows that it's completely optional and ask her if
she feels comfortable doing it. Most people will be flattered,
but some will feel like they've been drafted.

Be honest. Tell your bridesmaid why you chose her to be
in your wedding party—because she's important to you and
you just know you'll be friends for many years to come. (Right?
If not, maybe you should rethink her as bridesmaid material.)

Be understanding. If she seems less than enthused, ask
her why. It may be an issue you both can work out. For instance,
the problem may be a financial one. If so, you shouldn't necessarily offer to pay for her dress, shoes, plane ticket for the
wedding, or for boarding her cat while she's away—unless
you're totally loaded and she's completely and utterly broke.

But you should tell her you understand her hesitation and you will make every effort to choose items in her price range and will have a backyard barbeque shower instead of something fancy she'll have to chip in for. Hell, if she can't make it to the shower, that's okay with you too. I bet she'll come anyhow.

Now, don't say I didn't warn you. There will be a bad bridesmaid. Believe me. As fabulous and wonderful as your favorite girls are, there will be one who will be late making her payment to the dressmaker or who will refuse to have her hair done at your salon or who insists on wearing her own five-inch hooker heels instead of those beautiful silver peep-toes you picked out. Or maybe a few girls will each do one pain-in-the-ass thing. Or maybe they'll all be pains in the asses. No matter what, don't lose your cool. This is where the beauty of choosing the right maid of honor comes in. Pass the torch onto her (or someone else if you'd like) to play the bad cop. You shouldn't be the one stressing about this.

"My boyfriend's brother got married to a woman I didn't get along with. We could barely be in the same room together! When she asked me to be a bridesmaid, I burst into uncontrollable laughter. Then, I realized she was serious and muttered, 'Um . . . okay.' Awkward!"

—Marie

It helps if you learn to let go when it comes to some of the bridesmaid-y stuff. Oftentimes, our friends are happy for us but maybe a little bit jealous or afraid to lose our friendship when they find out we're engaged. Maybe they don't understand what the big deal about weddings is, or maybe they've experienced too many bridezillas and assume you're going to be the same way. Maybe they don't have the funds to buy all the things you demand and resent giving up their yearly vacation so that they can buy your mandated dress and shoes as well as get you a nice shower and wedding gift. Show your 'maids what a cool, non-zilla bride you can be. This might mean being more flexible than the typical bride. Instead of dictating the exact shoe style they should wear, give them parameters they might enjoy staying within. For instance, you can say, "Go ahead and choose any pair of shoes you want that's silver and has two-to-four inch heels," (to avoid the hooker shoes.) Hey, you might want to take it a step further and let the girls choose their own dress styles in the same color by the same designer. Some brides even let their 'maids wear whatever black dress they want so they can wear it again and again.

If I could go back in time, I would have been more relaxed when we "renewed our vows" in the church. Yes, I love my friends, brother, and brother-in-law and liked recognizing them by giving them the titles "bridesmaid" and "groomsman" but in all actuality, did I really need to force my friends to parade around in matching dresses they would have never otherwise chosen to wear and have the guys spend rental money at Men's Wearhouse? Probably not. I could have shown them we care about them by buying them a case of beer, a couple pizzas, and telling them they have no responsibilities for our wedding whatsoever. That would have gone over much better.

Now say you'd like to do some serious girl bonding on the wedding day and you'd like to make plans for everyone to get their hair done together at a salon. That's a totally sweet, nice, and fun idea. But don't expect everyone to go for it—not everyone enjoys shelling out their own hard-earned money to get their hair and nails done to *your* liking. Many will still agree to it, but if they don't have the dough or they don't trust hairstylists they've never used before—or if they're allergic to nail polish or something—you shouldn't force them to, unless you plan on paying for it. Then, do your updo dirtiest.

"My maid of honor sent me a 'Dear John' letter written by her mother the week before the wedding informing me that she was backing out. She sent along her bridesmaid dress. I haven't heard from her since."

—Melissa

Make sure you thank your bridesmaids on your wedding day. It's also customary to get each of them a gift. And for Pete's sake, don't *only* give them jewelry that matches the bridesmaids' dresses. That is cheesy, insensitive, and totally selfish! Get them something that they'll actually enjoy and use past your wedding day. If it's something small, in addition to something to wear for the wedding, that's totally okay.

SCANNER GUNS: VIDEO GAMES FOR WOMEN!

Unless you want to end up with a whole lot of crap to sell on Craigslist, you need to register for your gifts. And unless you want a bunch of questioning phone calls, it's best to decide where to register before the shower host sends out the bridal shower invites so they can include the information on the card. Whenever I get a shower invitation, I immediately go online, check out what the bride registered for, and plan out my gift. Inevitably though, I drag my feet too long and end up at a store the day before the shower getting the last three things on the registry and trying to figure out how they go together . . . a soap dispenser, a cocktail shaker, and pillow-cases. Hmmm, perfect for the bride and groom who are germ-phobes and like to make martinis in bed! But I digress.

Where you register and how much you'll need to register for will vary. If you're a young couple moving into your first place together, you'll need a house full of stuff and may even want to register in more than one store. On the other hand, if you've lived with your fiancé for a while, or you both have your own place that you'll be merging into one, you may only need some bath towels and fresh sheets.

Then there is the groom to consider. He may not be as thrilled as you to receive a Le Creuset Dutch oven from Williams-Sonoma and may want his and hers skis instead. Just avoid registering at too many places so you don't have store registry cards fall out of the invitation envelope like confetti. Remember, the wedding invitation should not mention anything about the registry or have store inserts, so the shower invites are the place to spread the news.

Registering can be very overwhelming, especially at a larger department or discount store where there are so many shelves and so many floors that you don't know where to start. If you're confused, here are my insider tips of what to register for:

- Eight place settings of everyday dishes
- Eight sets of everyday flatware
- Four-to-five pots and pans
- A bedding set: duvet, sheets, pillowcases, shams, bed-skirt

- Bath items, such as a shower curtain and soap dispenser
- Four sets of bath towels
- Area rugs or mats
- Home décor items such as picture frames, wall art, and shelves
- Small kitchen appliances, such as a toaster oven and crock pot
- Low priced electronics, like a handheld digital video camera

And here are a few things you might think twice about registering for:

- Any more than eight place settings, unless you have a large family and you entertain them often.
- China. Some couples find they use theirs a lot. Others just let the china collect dust. Give some serious thought to this.
- One of those boxed sets of pots and pans. They're usually pricey and include pots you don't really need, like the little tiny frying pans.
- Real silver flatware. Most department stores don't even sell this stuff anymore. It's not too popular since you can't put it in the dishwasher and it tarnishes. You'll probably have to special order it if you want it.
- Anything over $200. You might not get these really pricey gifts, unless some guests go in together to purchase them.
- One-use appliances that will take up space in your cupboards 364 days a year, like a juicer and a breadmaker if you rarely make juice or bread.

When you register, it's a good idea to take your fiancé with you. You two are making a home together, so you should both have a say about what chip n' dip trays and crystal nut bowls you want. Besides, registering for gifts is a blast! Just point, shoot, and receive. What a concept! It's Christmas every day when you have a scanner gun in your hand. My husband got scan-happy at the stores. Between that and my young enthusiasm, we ended up with a registry that was way too extensive. Yes, it sounds cool to put anything you ever wanted for your house on the registry, but the problem is that your guests will inevitably get you the offbeat stuff and ignore the things that you're more likely to use every day. I ended up with things like an egg slicer; that's useful right? Nope. Neither one of us has sliced even one egg with it. In fact, every time I see it in the drawer, it reminds me of the pretty napkin rings I could have received if only I didn't register for things like an egg slicer.

If your fiancé isn't into the idea of registering, don't force him to come along. Instead, bring along a friend who has excellent taste (even better if she's married and has been through this before), or your mom—as long as you and she usually see eye-to-eye on shopping choices. You don't want mom lecturing you on why you should register for that pretty floral dish pattern when what you really want is Fiestaware. But you should give your guy *something* that's his, so put a few of his favorite things on the list, like steak knives or whiskey glasses.

Cool places to register that you might not have thought of:

- **REI**—If you guys are outdoorsy and want to get camping, sports, and fitness gear, this is the choice for you.
- **Starwood Hotels**—If you're already planning a honeymoon at a Starwood resort (this is Westin, Sheraton,

Le Meridien, Luxury Collection, St. Regis, and W), you can register online for just about anything that's chargeable to a hotel bill, like spa services from the hotel spa, room service, or other resort restaurant meals. This is catching on with other resorts as well, so be sure to check and see if your honeymoon spot offers this service.

- **Target**—I love Target because not only can you find bathroom gear and kitchen appliances but you can also register for anything in the entire store including electronics, photo albums, and useful home stuff like a new steam mop. Those things are awesome.

- **Amazon.com**—Anything on the entire site is available to register for. It's not just books anymore: furniture, outdoor stuff, almost anything you can think of. And your guests can get free shipping on a lot of the items.

For more ideas, check out the Resource Section in the back of the book.

IT'S MY SHOWER AND I'LL CRY IF I WANT TO

It's finally your turn! After all the showers you went to, the gifts you bought, the small talk you've made, and the stupid games you've played, it's finally your turn to be the center of attention! Yay for you! But it's not all finger food and girly punch. Like the engagement party before this, you will have little or no control of the event and will even be told what to do. It may drive you crazy not to have the final say and bow to someone else's wishes. Now you know how your mother's been feeling these past few months helping you plan your wedding!

Usually it's the bridesmaids' responsibility to pow-wow to plan a shower. Sometimes, the duties fall upon the maid of honor or another friend or perhaps even a female cousin. Etiquette states that the only one who's forbidden to host the shower is the mother of the bride. The theory is that it's in bad taste for a mom to ask for gifts for her own daughter—which is what Mom being the host would mean. But most moms pooh-pooh this and still play a role in the planning. If you're a stickler for rules and are worried about someone thinking your mom hosting the shower is tacky, ask her if she'd mind if her name was omitted from the invites. Put your 'maids on there instead. She shouldn't be offended. In fact, my mom had my maid of honor make it a point to do that, and she's a real etiquette stickler.

Sometimes, too, there's more than one shower held in your honor. Perhaps your family may throw you one and your friends or co-workers may throw you another. It's okay to have two different showers with two different age groups or cross sections of people. In fact, your friends might have more fun at a coed shower held at a bar, but the older generation of relatives might feel more comfortable at a more traditional women-only event.

Although there are no specific rules that state when a bridal shower should take place, there are some guidelines. You don't want it within two weeks of your wedding date because you'll be scurrying around working out last minute details. And you don't want it more than four months before the big day since you don't really need your wedding celebrations taking up the better part of a year. About two months before is a good range of time, give or take a few weeks.

Showers range from daytime "girl only" fetes with dainty hors d'oeuvres, to coed evening bashes with a full bar. The personality of your shower probably will reflect the personality of your hosts. Once again, if you're digging on that coed theme but your friends have booked a frilly tea, you gotta go with the flow. Hey, you chose your friends, so if you're stuck at a women-only shower at a fancy social club eating sherbet and playing bridal bingo, it's your own damn fault. This is the brutality you must endure to get a new set of flatware and a wafflemaker.

WHO SHOULD BE INVITED TO THE SHOWER?

- Your mother and future mother-in-law.
- Any sisters and future sister-in-laws.
- Grandmothers.
- Women in the bridal party.
- Close female friends.

WHO SHOULDN'T BE INVITED TO THE SHOWER?

- Anyone you aren't inviting to the wedding.

WHO'S OPTIONAL?

- Extended family, if your fam is very large. If it's small, you should totally invite them.
- Your groom's extended family. But if you're inviting yours, you should invite his too.
- Kids. Kids don't need to be invited, but again, if you're inviting some people's kids, everyone else should have the option to bring theirs as well.
- Men and boys, unless you prefer to have a coed bash.

The Gifts That Keep On Comin'

A surprisingly difficult part of a shower is opening all the presents. Who would have guessed? Your guests try not to act bored as they watch the slow "conveyor belt" action: your bridesmaid hands you a gift, you open it, and give the bridesmaid the bow for the "bow-quet," you act surprised and exclaim how pretty/useful/practical/otherwise wonderful it is (this is especially difficult when you open your third set of salt and pepper shakers), hold it up for your friends to admire, pass it around, and have another bridesmaid take notes on what the gift is and who gave it to you for follow up thank-you cards. Phew! This is why I strongly suggest alcohol be mandatory at all showers. Not only so your guests can get buzzed while you open gifts, but also so that you can.

"My friends knew I liked playing laser tag so they surprised me with a laser tag shower. It was a good thought, but my older relatives just sat in the smelly holding room refusing to play, and had to eat really bad pizza that they were locked into ordering from the arena. I know my mom was embarrassed, which made me feel horrible."

—Jillian

Then there's always the inevitable "Yikes, I didn't register for this piece of crap" gift. Something that makes you discreetly gag as you realize that you must display the eyesore on your mantle for decades to come so the gift giver won't be offended when she comes over (usually when your mother-in-law drops by unannounced). If you're lucky and you get the gift from someone you don't know very well, cross your fingers that there's a gift receipt.

WHY ISN'T THERE A WOMEN'S VERSION OF *THE HANGOVER*?

Despite the fact that I haven't been to an engagement party, I've been to my fair share of bachelorette parties. The girls' night at a bar, the slumber party, the Atlantic City trip, the dinner with the bride's mom and sister, the '80s club, the fancy hotel room with a surprise stripper. Yep, I've been to them all, from rated G to triple X. And while bachelorette parties can be a blast, they can also be a dud, especially if you have some unexpected surprises.

If you haven't been to many bachelorette parties, let me warn you: sometimes they involve props. Your bridesmaids may pull out some crazy things, such as a silly sash or a fake veil, for you to wear while you're out and about. There will almost always be some props involving a penis in some way or another—I am amazed at how many party favors there are that are shaped like a penis. My personal favorite is a squirt gun. If your friends offer you props, I suggest you play along. It's all in good fun and you can deal with a little humiliation for one night of your life. However, it goes without saying that there are some places where props are inappropriate, like a fancy restaurant. At one party I went to, the maid of honor wanted all the girls to wear lacy garters over our pants and the restaurant wouldn't let us in with them. Personally, I wasn't disappointed.

Too much alcohol can be as much of a help as a hindrance. Boozing can really loosen some bachelorette party attendees up so much that they get along famously, even if they don't know each other. But sometimes it makes it even more awkward, especially if one group of friends likes to get drunk and grind on the dance floor and another group of friends is more of the sip and gossip about the girls grinding on the dance floor kind. Remember that alcohol reduces inhibitions and you certainly don't want to do anything, or anyone, that you'll regret in the morning!

> "We had a combo event of a shower and a bachelorette party. It sounded like a good plan until I found myself sitting in a room with both a giant fake penis and my mother-in-law. I thought I was going to die."
>
> —Jenny

Here are some common sense suggestions: Don't have your friends dare you to do all kinds of weird stuff like eat a banana seductively or have strangers "spank" you in the middle of the bar. It may seem innocent enough, but we live in an age where 80 percent of the public carries a camera cell phone and you don't want a video of you, no matter how innocent, showing up on YouTube. In addition, be sure to have a designated driver or go by cab or limo if you're planning to drink. And finally, don't stick a bunch of lifesavers on your shirt and let dudes suck them off. This is how swine flu is spread, people!

"Does getting kicked out of the club at your bachelorette party count as a good bachelorette party story?"

—Ana

If you're more of a low-key bride and are adamantly against a bachelorette party that involves penis props, drunken benders, and strippers that do inappropriate things to you, be very clear with your bridesmaids before they start planning the big event. Here are some more laidback ideas which will lessen the likelihood that you will have to untag photos of yourself the next morning:

Wine tasting—You don't have to go to Napa or Long Island; just have a fun party where everyone brings a different kind of wine to sample.

Spa trip—make dates for massages or pedicures. Just about every woman loves an excuse for a little pampering every now and again.

Cooking class—this can be a really fun way to break the ice between friends who don't know each other.

Knitting class—or just about any other craft class, unless you're extremely cynical.

Tour of a nearby brewery or art museum—Anywhere that offers free samples or something interactive to do is a good choice.

Karaoke night—I love those Korean karaoke bars where you rent a room so you only embarrass yourself in front of your friends, not a room full of strangers. Get some greasy Korean food beforehand.

The problem with planning something more complex than having a few drinks at a bar is that it can cost a pretty penny. And it can be wrong to ask your friends to keep shelling out big bucks for all these bashes surrounding your wedding. Especially at a bachelorette party where the other guests tend to offer to pay the bride's way, which can up the costs even more for your friends.

"My 'friend' asked to bring her 10-month-old baby to my bachelorette party. Did I mention that it was at a spa—with steam rooms and baths and the lot? Yeah, she is an ass. Thankfully, my friend who was organizing it (who is a mom to an 11-month-old) told her no way in H-E-double hockey sticks and offered her partner as a babysitter."

—Jenna

If you're looking for some lower cost versions of high concept bachelorette party ideas, get creative. Think about how you can have fun without going out of town, staying in a hotel, or paying a professional for pricey services. Instead of taking a trip to the spa, everyone can bring their own nail polish and supplies and you can do DIY pedicures together. Instead of a big steak dinner, have a potluck at the maid of honor's house. Hell, have game night or movie night. Wear your pajamas, pop popcorn, and talk about boys like you did when you were a teenager. Just add plenty of margaritas. If there's anything to be learned from this chapter, it's that alcohol makes almost all of these parties better.

Remember that bachelorette parties are all in good fun. So whether you stay in with the girls or go out and drink from dildo shot glasses, have a good time. No matter what you do, keep in mind that it's not a good idea to do this the night before the wedding—a few weeks beforehand is a much better idea. That way, you're free to stay up too late and look exhausted the next day, or get so drunk that you can continue puking well into the next morning.

CHAPTER 8

Doom and Groom

Here you are, all the way to Chapter 8, and you've barely read ten words about the groom. This may be symbolic of what you're experiencing in your life right now. You've been so wrapped up in cakes and DJs and lace and tulle that you've been putting your relationship with him on the back burner . . . in someone else's kitchen! Or maybe it's that all this wedding stress is making the two of you clash worse than Rosie and Barbara, or Rosie and The Donald, or Rosie and . . . eh, you get the idea.

Forget those preconceived notions that the engagement period is filled with candlelight dates, hand holding, and spending your nights together laying in bed, all sweaty and post-coital, dreamily fantasizing about hearing him call you "his wife" and him, your "Big Hubs." Instead, you're plotting to make sure he doesn't get to pick out the tuxes (you saw that blue number he wore to his prom) and getting pissy with him for forgetting to unload the dishwasher when you're really upset that he's letting his mom walk all over you. And sex—well, you can't remember the last time you did the deed.

If your relationship with your fiancé is strained, you're not alone. Disagreeing, needing alone time, and even having cold feet are all a part of the wedding race. But if you keep focused, stay on track, and don't elbow the fella next to you, you'll cross the finish line and win the prize.

REMEMBER WHY YOU'RE THROWING THIS PARTY IN THE FIRST PLACE

When you're knee-deep in wedding doo-doo, it's easy to forget the big picture: that the whole reason for the big day is that you want to marry the cool guy next to you. The one who lets you control the remote after football season ends and sleep in his favorite T-shirt that you love because it smells like him. If you're guilty of losing perspective, it doesn't mean you're a bad person; it just means that things like peony bouquets and gold-rimmed china have lured you over to the dark side of wedding planning. And this can happen to anyone, hey, it happened to Carrie Bradshaw and Mr. Big . . . although, to be fair, they are fictional characters.

Moving over to this dark side isn't good for your relationship. Showing your guy that he's not as important as seating charts and Dom Perignon can cause him pangs of resentment that will last a long time. It can set a precedent that it's okay to neglect him, and he you. Or worse, it can alienate him so badly that he questions why he's marrying you in the first place.

To avoid this, be sure to keep things in perspective. The reason for the wedding is that you're committing to sharing your life with this wonderful man and bringing your families and friends together to celebrate with you. It isn't about the silk gown or the candelabra centerpieces or the linen napkins. In fact, it isn't even about this one day. It's about starting the rest of your life as a team, side by side. And you being controlling or bossy or neglectful isn't the way a team works.

Once you've reminded yourself of this fact, be sure to do it over and over again. Also, make an effort to put the emphasis back on your relationship. Here are a few ideas to help you do just that:

Have date night. Make it a point to do things with your guy that aren't related to the wedding. While you're out mini golfing or dining on sushi, don't bring up the planning or problems that go with it. Talk about something else.

Give him some to-dos. You'll have less stress if you ask your guy take on a few wedding planning responsibilities himself, like finding a caterer or mailing the save-the-dates. Entrust these duties to him completely, without coaching—and don't second-guess or complain about his decisions afterwards. After all, this wedding day belongs to *both* of you.

Spare him some details. Even if you're pissed about the bridesmaid who insists on hemming her dress ultra-short, maybe your guy doesn't need you to go complaining to him for the 100th time. Instead, call up your best girlfriend or your mom and vent. Yes, your man should be a sounding board when you're upset, but if you use him as one *every* time, his patience for it all could wear thin—and rightly so.

Resist the urge to act like Bridezilla. Remember when you were little and people told you to count to ten before you reacted to stuff? This can still work at your age. You find out that your venue will *not* allow you to serve red wine and you must have it? Stop and count to ten. Think about how you want to deal with the issue before flying off the handle. Create a new strategy: either you give up the dark *vino*, you find a compromise (let guests drink it on the terrace but not indoors), or you find a new venue that will allow your favorite drink. In the end, your guy will admire your ability to work through the problem, not wonder whether you're going to act like a whiny bitch long past the wedding day.

> "My husband wanted our wedding to be in the back of his parents' barn and I wanted it to be at a nice hotel. We couldn't compromise and always fought, so we ended up eloping. We both figured no day was worth all that damage our fighting was doing."
>
> —Donna

In the end, it takes self-control and self-awareness to not alienate or neglect your guy. Show him how important he is to you, and I'm guessing he'll appreciate it.

TOP TEN WAYS TO GUARANTEE YOU'LL BE LEFT AT THE ALTAR

1. Obsessing about the wedding. How happy would you be if your fiancé rattled on about his obsessions with things like sports, beer, and Megan Fox?
2. Putting down his family and friends, no matter how crazy they're acting. Vent to someone else. He knows his peeps are flawed but it's offensive to hear about it from a third party.
3. Pooh-poohing his opinion each time he offers it. Granted, the guy thinks wearing a clean T-shirt is

dressing up, but planning a wedding should be a partnership.

4. Scheduling your wedding day for the Super Bowl, Stanley Cup Playoffs, or some other must-see sporting event. 'Nuff said.

5. Nagging and nitpicking. This will only remind him of his mother. And associating yourself with his mother can only do bad things to your relationship . . . especially in the bedroom.

6. Otherwise Bridezilla-ing. Seriously, do you want to be that girl?

7. Withholding sex until he agrees to the more expensive flower arrangements. Sex is not a weapon and will only make him want to withhold doing household chores to try to compete.

8. Inviting your maid of honor to register for gifts or leaving him out of some other duties normally reserved for the groom—unless, of course, he's asked you to.

9. Treating every setback as a major crisis. See "Obsessing about the wedding" above.

10. Choosing the engagement photo in which he's blinking to put on your save-the-dates because you look amazing in it.

HOW NOT TO BREAK UP BEFORE THE WEDDING DAY

You don't need me to tell you that there are approximately 2,437 decisions to be made along the way to the altar. And in order to make a decision, you need to form an opinion. Then you need your fiancé to do the same. With any luck, you'll agree. But often times, you won't. My husband really wanted our guests to throw rice at us after the ceremony like he saw at another wedding. As much as I tried to explain that rice kills birds, and could stick into my updo, he didn't believe me. Another topic ripe for disaster: you have your heart set on writing your own vows (it's so sentimental and sweet), but he gets stage fright and would prefer to go scripted. Listen, if you agreed on everything, there'd be something wrong. Arguing and disagreeing are to be expected along the way. It's how you deal with it that can either make you closer or pull you apart. When you're about to explode like one of those science fair baking soda volcanoes, take a breath, count to ten, and then follow my advice.

Don't:

Pout. You are not four years old and this really doesn't work. Plus, it's a total timewaster waiting for him to "come around" when he might never cave. There are persistent guys, too, ya know.

Throw things. It might seem like something feisty, impassioned people do as a release, but this will get you nowhere—except maybe having the police come to your door and losing that precious new set of dishes you got as a shower present.

Manipulate. Few of us are capable of *Desperate Housewives*–like deviousness. Instead, we just act like spoiled brats and find that people stop their conversations whenever we enter the room (yup, they *are* bad-mouthing you).

Refuse to give up. When you fight tooth and nail about every last detail of the wedding, you're just being a bitch. Learn when to let go.

Remember, the engagement period is like a trial run for the marriage. This isn't the only time in your lives when you two will be stressed, trying to make an impending dead-line, or disagreeing. Set the precedent now for respectful and kind conflict resolution.

Do:

Repeat. When your guy is expressing his point of view, show that you're actually listening and considering it (even if you're faking). Say something like, "I understand that you feel very intimidated about sharing personal feelings in pub-lic but it's important to me that we write our own vows because . . ."

Use "I" statements. Remember in sixth grade when we were taught not to point the finger all the time but rather to explain our own opinions and feelings? It might not have worked with the middle school bully but I bet it will now.

Focus. Don't make this fight about something else. Just because he doesn't want to write his own vows should not mean you should argue about how his mother never taught him to express himself—or how he's not mopping the floor enough, for that matter.

Compromise. What's the middle ground? There's usu-ally some you can find. For instance, maybe you guys use the traditional vows but tweak them slightly to be a little more personal. Or, you do write them, but you do it together and he's allowed to read his off a card, so it's less intimidating.

Bargain. I'm not saying to trade sexual favors for get-ting your way (as effective as that might be!), but maybe he'll agree to do the self-written vows if you say he's off the hook for doing a spotlight "first dance" at the reception.

Blame an outside party. I was saved from rice throwing by my venue's restriction on confetti and other messy things. It also might help to have one of his friends or relatives casu-ally bring up how they think rice throwing is tacky.

THE PRE-GAME PLAN

While you and your fiancé are indeed a team, chances are you're the team captain when it comes to planning your wedding. And while you certainly want to win, you don't want to make a foul or get a penalty or whatever other lame sporting references I can make before the big game. Here are some common situations that may rear their ugly heads in the game of wedding planning, and how you can tackle the problem:

He doesn't like the things you've planned or want to plan. As I mentioned before, this wedding belongs to *both* of you. You may think that because you have been dreaming about this day for a long time, you should have your dream bash to a tee, but guys sometimes fantasize about their wedding too, even though they will never, ever admit it. You don't want to plan an event that's so stuffy that your normally easygoing guy feels uncomfortable, or get married on the beach when he is prone to sun poisoning. The wedding is a reflection of who the two of you are as a couple. Communicate your wants and desires, but listen to him, too. You never know, he might have some decent ideas.

He doesn't want to help with the planning, but you're overwhelmed. Some men honestly don't give a rat's ass about weddings. But a lot of them do. They just don't know exactly what their role should be, or they're afraid to speak up because they think you won't listen to them when they express their opinions. If your guy is distancing himself from all the wedding-y stuff you're doing, and you're dying to have him lend a helping hand, approach him with some questions. Does he like white tablecloths or blue? Does he prefer strawberry cake filling or raspberry? Don't set him up for failure. Pick two things that you are honestly torn between and have him choose. Then take his opinion and use it. Build his confidence so he'll want to help out more. Then, maybe ask him to take care of a few things that are up his alley. If he's into music, for example, ask him to choose the reception playlist—but only if you're confident your guests won't end up stuck listening to four hours of Journey.

> **"At my wedding, my new husband stepped on the train of my dress multiple times, even though I kept telling him not to. Finally, it ripped. Why didn't he just listen?"**
>
> **—Christine**

He's irresponsible with his duties. He hasn't ordered the tuxes or reserved the rental car yet and the wedding day is fast approaching? Resist the urge to nag, lecture, scream, yell, or otherwise act like you're his mother. You are not his mother, nor do you ever, ever want to feel like you have to be in order to get him to do something. Instead, ask him nicely, as if you're not already well aware of his every move. "Oh yeah, whatever happened with the Mercedes you wanted to rent?" Make it seem casual. You have trusted this man to do this thing, and he is expected to do it. If you bring it up every single day, the likelihood he'll have done it diminishes. Express how excited you are about said Mercedes and how much you really hope you guys can get it since the rental company only has a limited number of them on the lot. Get him excited too, and watch the reservation get made. If that doesn't work, you can borrow my Toyota Matrix.

He won't tell off his parents/friends/others. It's unbelievably common for your future mother-in-law to be a complete pain in your ass while you're planning this shindig. And it's just as common for your future husband to do absolutely nada to remedy the problem. The only way I can explain it is that mothers and sons have a unique relationship. Boys . . . I mean men (I think), tend to have a whole hell of a lot of trouble recognizing when their moms are wrong. That can be really hard to accept. This guy is going to be your husband. He should be on your side. He should defend you when you're being victimized. However, it's your responsibility to ask him to do this; he won't just think of it on his own. Many men avoid verbal conflict or don't want to get in the middle of an argument. If it's worth a battle, ask him to take on this one. You two are a team and he should take one for the team every now and again. And if he says something to his mom/buddies/second cousins, they're more likely to back off.

"My mother-in-law gave us an ultimatum that she and her husband wouldn't even show up to our wedding if it was held in a church. (She's Jewish. I'm not.) We found a rabbi, at her insistence, and later she said he'd done a horrible job. Plus, she bad-mouthed my dress and didn't even give us a gift because we supposedly didn't include them enough in the planning."

—Meghan

BRRR . . . THESE TOES ARE CHILLY

"Cold feet." This clichéd term is not just a common plot for sitcom weddings, it's also a common problem for real-life weddings. Both you and your guy are ridiculously busy and way overstressed. You've got family and friends pulling you in different directions. You find that you're fighting all the time, and you're racing closer and closer to the day that you vow to spend the rest of your lives together. While the phrase "'til death do us part" may sound romantic to some, at this stage of planning, it just sounds creepy to you. You may see a side of yourself during this time that you haven't seen before, or worse, see a side of your fiancé!

If your feet area bit nippy, here's how to tell if they're something to worry about, or just warm up to.

THESE ARE EXAMPLES OF COMPLETELY NORMAL COLD FEET:

- You occasionally think that your fiancé is acting like a complete and utter asshole and every once in a while wonder why the hell you're marrying him.
- You find yourself fantasizing about the charming guy who sells you your morning latte.
- You begin searching for all your ex-boyfriends' Facebook profiles.
- You and your guy have been fighting more often than normal and you're worried it will never go back to the way it was before you got engaged.
- There's a passionate spark that you see gradually fading.

These are not examples of cold feet and are signs of a real problem:

- Your arguments turn violent.
- You can't find a compromise ever.
- You cheat on your guy or he cheats on you.
- The negative feelings last longer than four weeks.

If your cold feet are due to a real problem, you should seriously reconsider this marriage—you might be in love, but these are dangerous signs. Even if your cold feet are normal, it doesn't mean they should be written off as nothing. Seriously think about *why* you're feeling this way. If you can legitimately chalk it up to stress, then seek out some stress relievers (hello spa treatments!).

Even if you adore your man and know you want to grow old with him, marriage can still be a scary venture. We've all witnessed bad marriages and bad divorces, and we don't want that to happen to us. But there's a reason you said, "Oh my God, oh my God! Are you kidding? Oh my God! Yes!!!" when your boyfriend proposed. Instead of concentrating on all the frightening parts of marriage, concentrate on how to make yours strong from the get-go. Bond with your guy, communicate what you both want from marriage, and put in the work to keep those promises alive.

Usually, cold feet are just all the stresses and pressures involved in planning the wedding displaced onto the relationship. That's why it's crucial to focus on just the two of you. Go on a romantic weekend trip or have a good old fashioned makeout session. Remind yourself what you love about your guy.

If, on the other hand, he tells you that *he* has cold feet, you have less control over the situation. I know it's hard but try not to become immediately offended, hurt, and angry. As I mentioned before, this is a completely natural feeling and the fact that your guy is coming to you probably means that he doesn't want to be feeling it and is hoping you'll help him work it out.

> "I had cold feet before the ceremony, but then, the first moment I spent alone with my new husband was having him hold up my wedding dress so I could use the bathroom. We both laughed and I realized there wasn't a doubt in my mind that I wanted to spend the rest of my life with him."
>
> —Jeanie

Be understanding. Tell him all the reasons you want to be with him and remind him of all the things you've been hoping, planning, and dreaming about together. Explain that you, too, hope that nothing changes in your relationship once you're married, except that maybe you'll be even more devoted and committed to each other. Make sure you're still being you and not Bridezilla and that you're making time for him. If he's still feeling this way, consider talking to a counselor or therapist about your problems. Pre-wedding counseling is commonly offered by many pros, from clergy to therapists, for just this reason. Cold feet are something that are supposed to go away!

CH-CH-CH-CHANGES

Once upon a time, it was unheard of for the bride and groom to live together before they got married. That tradition seems outdated or prude now—so many couples seem to move in together around the time they get engaged. But be careful here because, as any expert will tell you, dealing with a major life change can send you into a downward spiral of emotional havoc, and getting married is enough of a change without throwing "moving in together" on the list.

If you're one of those couples that have been living together for a while, you've already adjusted to sharing closet space and toothpaste. But for the others, moving in together after you're engaged can be stressful, time consuming, and complicated. Living with someone you've never lived with before, no matter how crazy about him you are, is a tough adjustment. On top of that, while you're adjusting to the new living situation *and* planning the biggest event you'll ever plan, you'll be surrounded by boxes of ugly wedding gifts you can't exchange, piles of unassembled invitations and, well, all of *his* stuff. Talk about a recipe for a stressed-out, bitter, and feuding relationship!

So if you're planning a move while you're also planning a wedding, here's what I recommend for making the transition go as smoothly as possible:

Hire movers. I know DIY moves are so much cheaper, but you will feel such a weight lifted off your shoulders when you realize that you don't actually have to lift any weight onto your shoulders or bark orders at your well-meaning fiancé about where to put the 400 lb. pull-out sofa.

Plan ahead. Take out your planner and designate your free time the week before and at least three days after the move as devoted to moving and moving alone. No wedding planning tasks like vendor meetings or reception seating chart organization allowed. You'll seriously drive yourself nuts trying to go back and forth from task to task. And you'll be tempted to pull all-nighters, which aren't a good idea post-college.

Make room. Cut clothing closets and other storage spaces in half so you both have an equal amount of space to put your stuff. You don't want to start off your marriage with one person dominating the home. Yes, as much as you want to banish all his sports memorabilia to the basement, you really should let him have at least some of it out and about.

Keep the wedding room under control. Right off the bat, designate a space for the wedding planning paraphernalia. Don't let the homemade centerpieces you're making take over the house. Just as constantly talking about the wedding can get on your fiancé's nerves, constantly tripping over stuff for the wedding would be pretty damn annoying too.

Once you've moved in together, you'll have to adjust to sharing housework, closet space, and a tube of toothpaste, while still dealing with the stress of the wedding. That can be a lot to put on your relationship plate at once. It's important not to let the lines between domestic situations and wedding planning situations blur. Like, say, when you're frustrated that you have to cut your guest list in half because you can't afford 300 guests, and you take it out on your guy by screaming at him for accidentally deleting *The Bachelor* from the TiVo.

SEX AND THE ALMOST NOT-SINGLE GIRL

These days, not many of us are virgins who save ourselves for our wedding night. Usually, we're in the throes of passion some time in the early months of our relationship (okay, sometimes even in the early hours!). But once we get engaged, all that free time spent on foreplay disappears and the stress of wedding planning does a number on our libido.

"When we got back to our honeymoon suite, my husband had to pull 300 bobby pins out of my hair. It took forever and was a huge damper on the evening!"

—Beth

But remember, sex is a stress reliever. And, it's good for your relationship too, making you feel close to your fiancé and giving you both some fun, romantic, private time away from all the craziness of your family and friends and DJs with ponytails. Use these tips for keeping your sex life steamy while you're thinking about not-so-sexy things like reception chair covers and portable dance floors:

Have that all important date night. Date night = sex night. Forget all the thoughts and discussion about wedding planning for one night and think steamy thoughts instead. Capisce?

Keep all wedding planning related material out of the bedroom. This means no checklists that you fall asleep to as you make little pink checkmarks, and no laptop with the guest list in an Excel spreadsheet.

Do your at-home beauty treatments when your guy *isn't* home. I know you want to look your best on your wedding day, but nothing says sex buzz kill like a green mud mask, a plastic hair-dying shower cap, and girl-moustache bleaching cream. Keep some mystery alive.

Have first-dance-song tryout night. Add a bunch of sappy, sexy love songs to your iTunes list—Marvin Gaye and Barry White are highly encouraged—and tell your fiancé that you want to play them for him so you can find the perfect first dance song. Light a fire and some candles. Turn the lights down low. Crank it and dance. Let it lead to some horizontal dancing.

THE WEDDING NIGHT: CLIMAX OR COLLAPSE

If you thought the engagement period was unsexy, it's got nothing on the wedding night. Yep, I said wedding night. The one night you were convinced would be the steamiest, most intimate, and most orgasm-ridden of your life could very likely be a complete and utter dud. I've heard tons of stats about how more than half of married couples don't have sex at all on their wedding night. Usually it's because the bride and groom are too exhausted or too drunk. Sometimes it's because the after-party continues in the honeymoon suite and the couple can't get everyone to leave until the wee hours. For one bride I know, she and the groom were more interested in counting their monetary gifts than doing it (she later divorced—what a surprise). Another came back to the hotel only to find the room "decorated" by the grooms-men with toilet paper and latex condom balloons. The problem? She is allergic to latex. Nothing like a case of full body hives to ruin the mood.

Sure, your relationship will survive a wedding night without sex, but wouldn't you like your marriage to start out on the right toe-sucked foot? Here's how:

Avoid a white slip. This lingerie choice might be cute and bridal, but your guy might need the extra help going from exhausted to turned on. So go for something a little dirtier, like a red lace teddy or black garters and stockings. In fact, if he's looking for something to do to help plan the wedding, let him pick it out himself.

Drink in moderation. There will be tons of toasts on your wedding day. Because you're the bride, the waitstaff will probably be stalking you throughout the reception, constantly refilling your champagne glass, and it will be easy to lose track of how much you've had. And, because you may not get a chance to eat, you're even more prone to get drunk. Just put the glass down: you won't need to get loopy to have a good time on this day. Also, you'll be less likely to be in a wine fog when it comes time for the wedding night. The bonus? You'll feel less like a lush when you get the photos back from the photographer.

Keep your hotel a secret. I know a couple who lied and told all their family and friends they were staying in a completely different place than they actually were. This was to avoid any wedding night pranks or drop-in guests. I love the idea.

Head off your period. Yes, there is a way not to get it, but only if you're on the birth control pill. It has to do with skipping the placebo week of pills, but ask your doctor for more details and whether it's healthy for you to do this.

Sneak off early. The after party will be fun, so make an appearance if there is one, but don't stick around too long.

While no one's looking, slink away with your new husband. Don't worry—you won't miss much.

Get the room with the whirlpool tub. I have it on good authority that these are very, very sexy.

Don't take it too seriously. You may be envisioning the wedding night going down a certain way, but if your new husband has BO from break dancing to "Rapper's Delight," or you've got red indentations from your long-line bra all over your midsection, just laugh and go with it. And if for some reason it still doesn't work on the wedding night, know you've got the honeymoon to make up for it.

HOW TO HAVE A HOT HONEYMOON (AND I'M NOT TALKING ABOUT THE WEATHER)

Yep, you want the honeymoon to be romantic and intimate. This is not a family vacation—and it could be your last chance for quite some time to completely immerse yourselves in hanky panky. Sure, you've been stressed out for months and you'll be tempted to sleep it all off or to try to see all of Paris in six days (can't be done!) rather than bumping and grinding. But believe me, if you neglect sex on your honeymoon, you'll regret it. I can remember hanging out with another couple during our honeymoon. One night, the guys decided to stay up late and go to the casino while the other bride and I went back to our rooms and slept. Not sexy. Not sexy at all. If you want a hot honeymoon, I recommend:

Choose the right destination. While backpacking across Europe sounds like fun, you will be too beat from carrying that backpack by the time you get back to your hostel at night to do anything other than sleep.

Don't spend the entire day in the sun. Yes, a beach honeymoon is very hot and sweaty. But not between the sheets. Being in the sun all day is on par with lugging a backpack for sucking away your energy. If you go to the beach, make sure you incorporate some activity with basking in the sun—it's good for both you and your libido to not be so lazy.

"I didn't have my period on our wedding day (yay!) but we left for our European cruise a week later—and enter Mother Nature! Absolutely no sex on the honeymoon. Although, hitting seven cities in seven days is so exhausting, we were falling asleep during dinner ... so maybe we wouldn't have been up for it."

—Krista

Budget enough for a fancy hotel and nice dinners. We've all stayed in one of those motels that Oprah has done shows about. The kind where they shine a black light on the bed and expose a million stains. That's not the kind of place you should stay during your honeymoon. Even if you stay in a nice place, you should also spring for a romantic dinner. I know it sounds cliché, but it is totally a turn-on. Ordering aphrodisiacs like oysters and chocolates helps, but don't overindulge. Indigestion and food-induced comas interfere with sexy time.

Avoid over scheduling. Plan one day where you two stay in, order room service, and stay in the buff all day long.

Get the couple's massage. I once was lucky enough to stay at a luxury hotel that offered a couple's massage followed by a soak in a tub for two. Let's just say I highly recommend and leave it at that.

Mostly, the idea of keeping the peace with your groom is just a matter of working as hard on the relationship as you are on wedding planning (or at least keeping up the appearance that you are—let's face it: you're strapped for time and energy). Because after the wedding day is over, the thing you'll have to show for it is not only those beautiful photos from that amazing photographer, but your bond with him, too. You've got a whole lifetime of stressful, time-consuming moments to deal with. Make this practice.

CHAPTER 9

The Bride Diet (Hey, You Can Eat on Your Honeymoon)

I bet when you picture yourself on your wedding day, you imagine a gorgeous bride with flawless, glowing skin; a perfect, sophisticated coif; and an unbelievably hot hourglass figure. But then you look in the mirror and see the physical side effects that planning a wedding can render: dark circles under your eyes (from staying up late writing thank-you cards), scattered pimples (caused by stress), and a few extra pounds (due to snacking on comfort food). After all, you're only human, and who wouldn't show a little wear and tear while planning a major, havoc-riddled event?

Even if you defy the odds and show no ill effects, you still want to look your absolutely most fabulously best on your wedding day. This is the one day of your life where all eyes will be on you. You'll feel like the paparazzi is following you with all the flashes going off—and, in the pictures, you want to look more like Halle Berry at a movie premiere than Lindsay Lohan after a bender. That's why, with time still on your side, you'd better get a grip on your look.

WHY CAN'T WEDDING DRESSES COME IN "SLIMS YOUR ASS BLACK?"

When it comes to bridal beauty and fitness, you need to super-size your regular routine (aka: whip your body, skin, hair, and teeth into magazine-cover-worthy perfection with the clock ticking away because of your fill-in-the-blank date deadline). Sure, that means motivation, but it also means that you could fail miserably, the repercussions of which will be on display for all to see. Oh, and captured in a few thousand photos. Between diet, exercise, makeup, hair, and get-ready-for-the-big-day beauty treatments, you could end up spending a lot of dough, wearing yourself out and, hell, not being happy with the results. That's why I'm here to fill you in on the "don'ts" before you say "I do."

Shaping Up, Not Breaking Down

Our lives are already mega-busy, eh? Who doesn't have 7 A.M. to 11 P.M. booked solid for the next three months? Maybe there was a time when people sat on their porches and sipped lemonade for hours on end, watching the cars go by, but now the closest thing we get to having down time is sitting in bumper-to-bumper rush hour traffic. Every bride wants to look fit and toned on her wedding day, but there's no time to actually work out in order to *get* fit and toned.

I hate it when I complain that I don't have time to work out and someone tells me to simply *make* time. What they really mean is to cut out something fun in my life and replace it with the gym. It's not like we working girls get the option of less office hours, less time-consuming train commutes, or less non-quality time at our future mother-in-law's famous tension-ridden family dinners. Instead, you'll have to sacrifice this week's episode of *The Bachelor* or happy hour beers with your co-workers in order to have enough time to work out.

Cutting all the fun out of your life could make even Minnie Mouse want to slit her wrists, and you shouldn't do that. Instead, explore ways that burning some extra calories might actually be kind of fun. Why not try:

- Taking up a sport or revisiting one you played long ago. Think a little beach volleyball, tennis, or even a game of H-O-R-S-E. The more competitive you get, the more you'll work at it.

- Giving yourself rewards—guilty pleasures are a good idea (but not junk food). Ran five miles this week? You get to watch *I Didn't Know I Was Pregnant* instead of *NOVA* this weekend.

- Trying a new, challenging class. I'm not talking about a spin class where the instructor barks orders at you the whole time (unless you're completely warped and that sounds like fun to you) but something that sounds like a good time, like belly dancing, Zumba, or hip hop. You'll be so distracted by learning the moves that you won't be focusing on the fact that you're working out.

- Creating a playlist of awesome songs to work out to. Sounds like a no-brainer, but knowing that you'll get to listen to some favorite tunes makes working out less of a cross to bear.

On top of everything, you have a deadline for getting fit. In the not-too-distant future, you have a dress that needs to zip up. Plus, you're trying to get rid of arm flab and create things that resemble triceps so you can look amazing in your strapless gown in time for your nuptials. If you need help getting in shape fast, you might want to:

Hire a personal trainer. It goes without saying that these people know what they're doing more than you do. Point out your problem areas, and they'll show you how to do the right moves to target them. They'll also push you harder than you'll push yourself when you're on your own.

Take a boot camp class. These are available in most areas. Usually, it's a weekly or weekend-long class, designed like a military regiment. They're known to pack a lot of hard work into a short chunk of time. You'll be moving too quickly to realize how much you ache.

Kick your workout up a notch. Currently working out three days a week? Bumping it up to four can keep you from plateauing.

Combine exercise with a good eating plan. Make sure you're cutting calories from your diet and keeping a good balance of protein, carbs, and fat. Cut out all the bad stuff like soda, junk food, etc., and replace it with fresh fruits and vegetables, and be sure you're drinking eight glasses of water a day—that's key.

Rev up your metabolism by eating five to six smaller meals throughout the day instead of three large ones.

Once you start your workout routine and stop eating all the crap, you'll quickly learn that grouchiness and insanity ensue. Blame it on the absence of sugar in your diet and the presence of a 5 A.M. alarm that screams, "Get your running shoes on and your ass out the door—Pronto!" It's enough to drive anyone batty. Sugar and sleep help us deal with stress—at least momentarily—and when we're tired and overwhelmed, we feel worked to the bone. Luckily, the experts say that being physically fit can actually help you deal with stress better and make you feel more energetic *in the long run*. However, you have to struggle through the cinnamon-bun-deprived short run in order to get there.

It's important to take care of yourself so you can feel your best as you make this transition. I mentioned drinking lots of water; keeping hydrated is really important for your mood. So is making sure you're not starving yourself. Pack healthy snacks such as granola bars, trail mix, yogurt, and the like when you're out on vendor appointments and registering for gifts. That way, when your blood sugar drops dramatically, and you get all Cruella DeVille on your fiancé's ass, you won't be tempted to hit the mall food court or, worse, McDonalds for a quick Mac attack.

Now with all that running around, you have to find the time to actually run around . . . you know, in the shoes with the sports bra and the whole nine yards. Increase the likelihood of sticking to your goals by scheduling your gym rat time. Take out your Blackberry or iCal or date book and write it in the way you would a meeting with your caterer. Make sure you leave yourself enough time for the whole she-bang: getting to the gym, changing into the clothes, making it to your class or to your elliptical machine in time to watch *Entertainment Tonight* on the TV, showering, and getting home.

Learn to multitask. Instead of meeting your best friend for lattes, meet her for yoga class. Read your work reports while you're on the treadmill. Watch *The View* that you Tivo'd while lifting weights. Sign up for ballroom dancing with your guy—that's date night, first dance preparation, and a workout all in one. Now that's what I call multitasking!

Make getting to the gym as easy as possible. Join one that's close to your office or home, and be sure to always have an extra set of gym clothes on hand for after-work workouts. When there are a million reasons not to workout, it's easy to make excuses. Lessen those reasons.

"Three months before my wedding I joined a popular gym by my house. The only problem was that the parking was horrible. Sometimes I'd drive around and around looking for a spot, and end up at home eating cookies without stepping foot inside the gym."

—Sara

One of the excuses people make is the general cost of working out. It often requires you to sign a year-long gym membership contract, which means beaucoup bucks. And that can also mean investing in cute gym clothes so you can feel good while you're at step aerobics class, even though you'll sweat out a two liter of diet soda while you're there. It can also mean purchasing yoga mats, dumbbells, Wii Fit, and those weird electronic surge belts for abs that are sold on infomercials. Before you start investing, remember that there are plenty of ways you can work out without sacrificing your floral budget.

Cheap—and Free—Ways to Get Fit
Between the fortune you're spending on lilies and linens, you don't have a spare penny to spend on trainers and expen-

sive gym memberships. That's okay. It doesn't need to cost a muscular arm and a toned leg to get in shape. Here are some inexpensive ways to get ripped:

Visit your local park and do "the fitness trail." A lot of them have fitness equipment set up throughout. All you do is jog between each station and follow a posted guide to each workout. You'll be doing old school classic moves, like dips and pull ups.

Go swim in the ocean or the community pool. Swimming works crazy muscles normal workouts can't. That's why you're famished after you go swimming—and why Michael Phelps's body looks like it does.

I don't think I need to point out this one out but . . . tie on those shoes and get running in your neighborhood (who needs an expensive gym track when you have a sidewalk?). If you hate running, take a brisk walk. It's lower impact, but as long as you're hustling, you're burning plenty of calories and getting those leg muscles ready for all those short skirts you'll be wearing on your honeymoon.

Check out Craigslist or other local message boards. Find organizations that get together to bike, play field hockey, go sled riding—whatever! Sometimes there are also free yoga lessons in the park or something similar offered by your community or a teacher who's just starting out and trying to build buzz. Take advantage.

Join the work softball league—or kickball or whatever it is the people in your office do. So you'll have to deal with your co-workers' nonsense a few more hours a week, but at least you can discreetly laugh at how your boss' chicken legs look in gym shorts.

Check out the bargain bin. Workout DVDs can get expensive, but not if you're looking in the bargain bin. You can usually find some decent ones for under nine dollars. Also, check out iTunes for free and affordable fitness podcasts. They're easy to download and if it's free, you've got nothing to lose but a couple pounds off your ass!

BEAUTY IS A BEAST

If you ever needed an excuse to hit the spa and beauty salon, you have one now. You've got sore muscles that need to be rubbed, roots that rival those of giant redwoods, and blackheads out the wazoo . . . and your videographer is shooting in HD! It's time to prep for the camera, my friend, because you have to be ready for your close up.

As wonderful and pampering as beauty treatments may sound, there are some drawbacks to all that primping. For one, spa treatments are ridiculously expensive. They're also not an exact science. I mean, how many times have you left the salon with highlights that were too blond or bangs that were way too short? You don't want to leave this stuff up to chance or the will of the beauty gods.

To prevent the "unnatural" look, you need to make a beauty plan. I know that sounds like some lame thing high school girls who carry Coach purses would say, but it takes a lot of effort to look effortlessly fabulous. Decide what about your present look you'd like to preserve and what you'd like to subtly improve upon. This means abiding by a few golden rules:

Beware of doing something radical. Don't become a brunette when you've been a blonde for the last fifteen years. You want to look like yourself on your wedding day. The only exception is if you're going back to your natural color, know you'll like it, and plan to keep it that way for at least a few years.

Don't do anything permanent. I'm talking eyeliner tattoos or—hell, this is the twenty-first century—plastic surgery. I know there's this urge to be a triple D to fill out your wedding dress, but I don't recommend satisfying it, Barbie. You need time to heal—for some procedures it takes months for the swelling to go down—and to know that you like your new look. I would hate for you to have obvious collagen in your lips in your wedding pictures.

Whatever you do, do not spray tan, unless you've tested it out plenty of times beforehand. Yup, how to avoid looking like a Cheeto is a lesson learned from MTV's *Jersey Shore*. Even a color that's just a little off can look even more drastic in wedding pictures, and it's really tough to get even results. The only way to guarantee that you'll avoid funny streaks is by not doing it. No matter your skin tone, you will still look amazing in that white dress.

Tread lightly when trying something for the first time. It would be ridiculous to get your hair cut in a bob three weeks before your wedding if you don't know for sure whether or not you look good in a bob. Also, if you don't know how your skin will react to a facial, plan ahead so you have enough time for a couple trial runs.

Your beauty plan should include everything you want to try, whether it's waxing, a pedicure, hair color, a facial, or something else. Just know when to schedule it in relation to your big day. The last thing you want is to refuse to let your groom lift your veil because it's hiding your scary residual red face from a chemical peel. Here are some general guidelines:

Facial

A facial is customized to your skin type. It can be designed to get rid of blackheads and pimples or to remove layers of dry skin. Get this done a few months before your wedding to see how your skin handles it. Many people break out right after a facial, especially if they've never had one before, so pay attention and plan accordingly. Follow your aesthetician's advice about how often to get this done—she might suggest once a month, but you can probably swing every six weeks or so. This will lessen the likelihood of unplanned adverse reactions. Then, plan to get your final pre-wedding facial about a week before the big day to allow any post-facial blemishes to fade.

Massage

With every rub and knead, you'll feel your mother-in-law's critical voice fade quietly into the background. You don't need me to run down the different types: Swedish, shiatsu, hot stone, reiki, etc. Ask your spa what they offer and choose whatever sounds good to you. I highly recommend having one done a month before your wedding. It will give you an excuse to escape stress for an hour or so of your life. It will also allow you to check out the results, because if you have very sensitive skin, you might get temporary red marks from an overzealous massage therapist. If that's not the case, schedule one for the day before your wedding to de-stress.

Teeth Whitening

There are some really cool teeth-whitening procedures you can get done by your dentist or a company like Brite Smile or Zoom. If you have major stains on your teeth and you've been meaning to get this done for a while now, I say go for it. But make it a point to talk to the dentist in advance so he doesn't go too far. No one wants a mouth full of Chiclets to mock them in their wedding photos. These results last about a year, so I say schedule it about a month before your nuptials.

Facial Waxing

If you plan on getting any facial hair waxed—eyebrows, upper lip—I highly recommend that you use a professional. Although it may sound trivial, if someone screws up your eyebrows, your whole face could look a little off kilter. If you don't have a professional you trust, get that all important personal recommendation. Try out a few different providers until you find one that's right for you. Then, plan to have your facial hair waxed a few days before the wedding. Never do this the morning of the wedding—you'll have redness and maybe a little bit of puffiness from the wax and oils.

Bikini Waxing

A bikini wax can make you feel extra confident on your wedding night and in a bitty bathing suit on your honeymoon. It can also make you feel a great deal of pain. My own lone bikini waxing experience is a close second to my childbirth experience as the most painful thing I've ever gone through, but lots of women love to get the hair on their hoo-ha ripped out by the root on a regular basis. If you want to try it for the first time, pop an aspirin before the procedure to help you get through it. Do a trial run about two months before the big day to see if you have any issues with resulting ingrown hairs, then have the next one about a week before your wedding day. Supposedly, the more often you do it, the less painful it becomes. Traumatized by my own experience, I've never made it back to the waxer and instead have invested in a good razor.

Hair Coloring

If you plan to slightly change your color or try a new type of coloring (semi-permanent as opposed to permanent), you'll prove to be a really smart chick if you try it out a month or two in advance and then get a touch up about a week before your big day. As anyone who has ever dyed their hair knows, the color can look different right after it's done as opposed to after a few washings. So be strategic. This is especially true for treatments like highlights, which can look different every time you do them (they tend to get progressively lighter every time).

BARGAIN BASEMENT BEAUTY

Of course, you may be reading this section and simultaneously cursing me under your breath. Now that I told you what the beauty magazines will tell you, let me also say that you don't have to get all this stuff done by professionals. Do it if you can afford a little splurge here and there, but there are plenty of products you can use at home and get quality results. For example:

Microdermabrasion Kit

Microdermabrasion procedures at a spa or dermatologist's office are meant for evening your skin's texture and tone. If you're looking for a substitute, a beauty editor at a women's magazine once told me that most microdermabrasion at-home kits are pretty good. Usually, they involve a facial scrub or gentle brush—sometimes even an electronic brush—that sloughs off the top layer of skin to reveal the newer layer down below. It won't give you as dramatic results as the spa (which in turn won't give you as drastic results as a dermatologist), but you should see a difference. Just be sure to pick a product by a maker you trust—I like the Mary Kay kit—and use it as directed, with all the lotions and tools meant to go with it.

"I thought I'd use the free makeup application at the beauty counter on my wedding day, but after the trial run, I was wiping layers of gaudy purple eyeshadow and fluorescent pink lipstick off my face. I figured the Krusty the Clown look was out, so I'd just do my makeup myself."

—Amber

Waxing Kits

If you have a high pain threshold and don't mind inflicting it on yourself, try out an at-home wax. Bikini, legs, and underarms are good places to wax on your own. The upper lip is okay too, but I like to leave the eyebrows to a professional. If you're a complete wuss like me, don't worry. Unless your legs resemble Robin Williams' back, you don't need to get your legs waxed. A close shave will do the trick.

White Strips

Those at-home whitening strips actually give great results and can lighten your teeth a shade or two. They won't get rid of particularly extreme stains, but can do the trick if you just need some subtle brightening. I also find that whitening toothpaste gives good results and there's no extra stuff to remember to do.

Hair Dye

If you're a dye out-of-the-box girl and always have been, there is no reason for you to suddenly start getting professional hair coloring. You know what color you like. You know how to do it right—a.k.a. being sure you get every strand and knowing how long to leave the color on for. If you've never had your hair colored before though, go see a pro. Someone who knows what they're doing can really work with you to get the results you're looking for—and can talk you out of what seems like a bad idea, like those violet highlights with your olive complexion.

HAIR TRIALS AND TRIBULATIONS

Even the women with the most simple beauty routine—comb hair, brush teeth, moisturize, go—wear makeup and style their hair on their wedding day. Of course, the prospect of having your hair done by a pro means completely entrusting the way you look to someone else. You risk streaky blush and a poofy 'do. You also risk messing it up, which is easy to do if you're not regularly attending red carpet events and not used to having lots of creams and powders and potions on your face. Chipped nails, lipstick on the teeth, and stray confetti embedded in an elegant coif are all things that brides fear.

The good news is that it's customary to schedule a trial run for both hair and makeup if you're having them done professionally. If you're DIYing or entrusting this to a beauty savvy friend or relative, also be sure to do a trial run—and you might want to make it two trial runs in this event.

I'm sure you have at least a vague idea in mind for how you want your hair to look. If not, I suggest going to your favorite gossip rag or website and looking at red carpet photos for ideas. Instyle.com even has a feature where you can "try out" different celeb 'dos on a picture of your face. Look for something classic and elegant—because an overly trendy look will be something you'll regret when you look at your photos a decade from now. I love the idea of a chignon or other very neat, tight hairstyle, too, since curls and loose updos tend to get messed up during spirited dances to "YMCA." You just need a whole helluva lot of hairspray to keep the chignon in place.

Once you've got some ideas, tell your stylist exactly what you want, and express any uncertainty. You want to work together to combine your vision and her expertise. For example, she may discourage you from a specific style if it's not quite right for your face shape, hair type, or skin type. At the trial run, you'll fine-tune the look for your big day.

Tips for the Hair Trial:

Seriously, schedule it. Some hairstylists will charge you extra for this sitting and as tempting as it is to save a little dough, do it. Peace of mind is totally worth fifty dollars. About a month before the wedding day is a good time to lock down this time. Make sure your "hair look" is done so that the color and cut will be the same as it will be on your wedding day. You can still fine-tune any details, such as exchanging those crystal butterfly clips for a stylish headband.

Come prepared. Bring your veil, tiara, headpiece, barrettes—whatever you plan to wear on your head on the big day. If you would like to take the veil off post-ceremony, be sure you see what the 'do will look like with and without it.

Take advantage. If you're trying to decide between two different looks, have her style both on you. Also, do different variations, like say, a side part and middle part. It's one thing to say, "Oh let's do this but a little bit differently on the wedding day," and an entirely different thing to actually see that finished product and know that it's your best bet.

Heed any warnings. If you've gone to a pro and she says you're hair is too short or thick or curly or straight for a certain style, listen. They tend to know what they're talking about, and you don't want your French twist to gradually unravel throughout your wedding day. Try another look instead.

During these trial sessions, you really want to communicate what you like and don't like about what the stylist is doing. Take pictures so you remember it—and so you can look back on the days leading up to the wedding day and double check that it's exactly what you wanted. The same goes for the makeup trial.

Tips for makeup that doesn't suck:

Be time sensitive. A daytime wedding look is a lot different from a nighttime wedding look. The same goes for a spring and a winter bash. Be sure your makeup colors properly reflect that. If your daytime wedding is going to go into night, consider a more natural look for the first part and apply something more evening appropriate after the ceremony.

Say no to shine. There are some really pretty, dewy looks you can create using powder and lip gloss that have shine to them, but save those for another day. Camera flashes tend to reflect the light of those shiny things and create white spots in the pictures, so stick with matte and get some of those anti-shine papers that you press on your skin. Those things work.

"During my hair trial, the stylist suggested I try out some hair extensions. After I said okay, she brought me these long, dark, wavy, ratty-looking things. I spontaneously burst into tears. Smart lady: she hid those things fast."

—Karen

Get free advice. If you're doing your makeup on your own or having a friend help you, head to the makeup counter first for a free color consultation. The makeup counter peeps can be slightly annoying—and they'll try to push you to buy their products, but you don't have to. Pay attention to the way they apply the makeup and the types of colors and formulas they recommend for your skin type and coloring. You can get lots of good ideas this way.

Go waterproof. Use as many waterproof products as you can. Lady Gaga may be able to pull off the raccoon look, but alas, the rest of us cannot.

Remember to maintain. On the wedding day, make sure you pack, at the very least, the powder and lipstick that you're wearing. Eye makeup and some blush are good ideas too. Make it a point to head to the ladies room every hour and a half or so to check on the status of things. You don't want a little smear or crease to make you hate your wedding photos.

Sure, pain is beauty and beauty is a f%$#ing pain, but I've heard from so many women that they were glad they lost those five extra pounds or sprang for the professional makeup artist on their wedding day. Listen, you don't want your wedding photos to end up in the bottom drawer where you stash your old school photos and pictures not worthy enough to place in actual albums.

CHAPTER 10

The Devil's in the F^$#ing Details

You've got the venue, the gown, the bridesmaids' dresses, the tux, the car, the florist, and all that other big stuff out of the way. Your to-do list is full of checkmarks and you're giving yourself little pats on the back left and right. You're almost there! You're still alive, still engaged despite your fighting, and still hate your mother-in-law (some things will never change!). You even have a little bit of sanity left! You're home free! Right? Well, not so fast.

The final weeks before the wedding day can be pretty tough. You could have been planning this damn thing for the past *year* and still not be ready for the details you haven't thought of and the spit-covered curve balls that will be thrown your way. The weeks leading up to your nuptials will be filled with things to do that aren't even on your to-do list. Things that are tedious and things that require ultra-organization, as well as communicating with difficult people, heading off fighting and dissatisfaction from said difficult people, and, well, predicting what will happen on the soon-to-be most unpredictable day of your life thus far.

ISN'T BUYING 204 FILET MIGNONS ENOUGH TO SHOW YOUR GUESTS YOU CARE?

After years of writing about clever wedding favor ideas, I have a confession to make: I think favors are pretty lame. The idea of giving your guests a gift to thank them for sharing in your big day is actually really sweet, but the reality is not. Take the amount of money that brides have to spend on wedding favors and divide it by 300 or 150 or 80 or however many guests you'll have, and you're bound to be scouring the Dollar Store or Wal-Mart in search of "something nice," to no avail. I've been at those weddings where snobby people are eyeing the cute bag of Hershey Kisses with a critical eye, wondering why they didn't get Godiva, but the truth is, that bride probably spent $300 on those Kisses!

And then there are those knickknack favors—the little candle, the mini picture frame (I am guilty of this one), and a wine glass filled with little hand soaps. These are nice ideas in theory, but most of us need more chotchkies to clutter our homes like we need a hole in the head. No one needs a candle that will burn for five minutes, a wine glass that doesn't match the ones at home, and unless there's a grade-schooler at home, a damn wallet-sized photo frame. And once you've taken off the price tags and slapped a monogrammed sticker on them, there's no returning the extras that are left to Dollar General. Unless you want your home filled with fifty-seven heart-shaped boxes, these general guidelines might help:

Go useful. I have a friend who's always talking about the salad tongs she got at a wedding as a favor and how she uses them all the time. There will, of course, be those guests who already have a drawer full of salad tongs or who don't eat salad at all that won't love them, but you can't please them all.

Think edible. Treats you can eat usually don't get left behind, since most guests eat them right then and there or save them for the ride home. If you're going to buy cookies or candies, don't just go for something cute, make sure you get a sample and *taste* them before you order 300 of them. Believe me, I sampled a million custom sugar cookies from wedding companies and most of them tasted like paste. Or instead, try M&Ms in your wedding colors. Not only are they affordable, but everyone likes M&Ms!

Avoid overspending. There are tons of favor ideas out there for three dollars-a-pop and under. Those brides who decide they want to get everyone a designer soy candle that cost twenty dollars have the best intentions, but most guests don't know who the hell Jo Malone is and half of them will complain that the scent irritates their allergies.

Make it personal. If you're really into wine, give guests a cool corkscrew, or if you met your groom while skiing the Alps, give everyone a pretty mug with cocoa mix and marshmallows. People like stuff with a story. You might even write a little tag with the meaning behind the favors and attach it to the package.

Don't go too custom. It's really sweet to personalize the favors by putting a pretty tag or stamp on the packaging with your monogram, photo, or wedding date on it, but do not give guests a mug or frame engraved with all your wedding info on it. The same goes for coasters with your picture on them. These are all things your parents might treasure, but not your boss or your third cousin twice removed. The trinkets you spend a hundred bucks on will be likely be banished to the back of their closet.

Do it serve-yourself style. Put together a buffet of candy, cookies, coffee beans, whatever you like. Leave bags and scoops so everyone can help themselves to the stuff they want. It's a fun activity for the reception, and whoever doesn't want any simply won't take them.

Consider nixing the favors altogether. Chances are, people won't miss them. Hey, they're already drinking your booze and dining on a meal you've provided. Spend the extra money on additional hors d'oeuvres or another hour of music, something they'll truly appreciate.

Be charitable. If you're worried people will notice your lack of favors or if you just want to do some good, you might want to donate to charity. Wouldn't you rather benefit someone who really needs it than spend lots of money on stuff people throw away anyhow? It's especially nice to give to a cause that's near and dear to your heart. Let everyone know about it by leaving cards that describe the cause on the tables or near the guest book and say that a the donation has been made in guests' honor in lieu of wedding favors.

Once you get the favors out of the way, you'll have to order (make sure they'll come in at least ten days before the wedding), assemble, pack, and store them. All of these things are pains in the ass. Many brides like to get cute and pick fancy paper to wrap their favors in. This can make them look nice sitting on the dinner tables at the reception. If this is what you want to do, go right ahead—it makes the favors seemmore special. But do not attempt to tie 247 polka dot ribbons yourself. Instead, plan a favor-making party with your closest girlfriends—you know, the ones who don't mind if you use them for free labor from time to time—and supply lots of Oreos and vodka. Also, consider placing the favors on a table near the exit of the reception. Guests are less likely to forget them if they're on their way out.

OUT OF TOWNERS = OUT OF YOUR MIND

For your in-town guests, there isn't much more for you to do than plan the wedding and dole out those favors you agonized over. But the out-of-towners can be high maintenance. As the RSVPs start rolling in, so do endless questions and requests for things like where to find a good vegan restaurant, tickets to a show while they're in town, and a good babysitter to watch little Lulu during your bash.

I will say this now, with emphasis, because it will make you feel much better: *You don't have to pay for out-of-towners' hotel rooms, pick them up at the airport, or entertain them throughout the wedding weekend.* If anyone believes that I'm wrong, they should be promptly smacked upside the head. I don't care how close/far/nice/bitchy/young/old/broke the person, they should not guilt you into paying their way or letting them stay on the pull-out bed in your wedding night suite. But they may try. If they do, point out the wonderful things you've done in advance to make their lives easier over the weekend. They can include:

Blocking Hotel Rooms
If you're having the reception at a hotel, you'll naturally coordinate with your venue. If not, find a hotel or two

nearby where you think guests will want to stay. Some couples choose a more luxurious option and a cheapie, so guests who prioritize comfort and price differently can all be happy.

"Blocking" rooms basically means that the hotel will set aside some of their rooms expressly for your guests, as long as they book by a certain date—usually a few weeks before your event. Often, they'll give your guests a discount on a standard room, as long as they say they're with your wedding or give some sort of a code during booking. Guests like feeling as though they're getting a good deal even if it's, like, ten dollars off the normal rate.

If you've never stayed in that particular hotel before, ask if you can tour one of the rooms, just to be sure it's nice and not cockroach-ridden. Ask if the hotel will actually block all your guests together in one part of the building if you "room block." This is fantastic if you've got a fun bunch that loves lots of togetherness. Not as fabulous if you've got two crowds that won't quite mix. After my wedding, some guests' late-night hotel room rowdiness had to be broken up by a visit from the local police. Thank God my grandparents-in-law weren't staying next door. Most couples block hotel rooms before the invitations go out so they can put details inside the envelopes, but you can do this at any time and spread the word.

Booking Transportation

If you've got out-of-towners flying in for the festivities, they'll be concerned with getting from place to place. While it's not your responsibility to pay for their transportation, you should provide them with information. If they're staying close to the airport, see if their hotel provides a shuttle bus. If they need to rent a car, find out where a car rental service is located. Most all airports are close to rental car companies that offer shuttle services, but it is more expensive to rent a car from an airport location. If your guests have children, let them know that many car rental companies offer car seats for a minimum fee. Then there's always the airport taxi, as well as public transportation. If they are using public transportation, find out the schedule from the Internet and e-mail the link to your guests.

The only exception to the "not paying" thing is if your guests are staying at the hotel where you've blocked rooms, you might offer to provide transportation from the hotel to the ceremony and reception, then back again. The hotel's shuttle bus can usually be booked for a small extra fee. If not, look into a local limo rental company and see what kind of "party buses" they offer. These are usually nice coaches that everyone can feel comfortable climbing aboard. They don't need to be big enough to fit all the out-of-towners, since they can make several trips back and forth throughout the evening. Plus, guests can leave when they want and not wait around for everyone else to call it a night. Providing this transportation is definitely *not* a must, but it really cuts down on the potential for drunk driving and bridesmaids wandering around town after midnight. I've been on some fun shuttles complete with sing-a-longs. To be sure everyone is aware what time the last shuttle will leave the reception, provide that info in the guest gift bags. Which is a perfect segue to . . .

The Gift Bags

You don't need to go crazy and spend half your budget on these pretty little parcels, but you should pack up a few essentials for your guests and give them to the hotel concierge to hand out. This will make arriving at the destination after their long travels feel that much better.

When guests check in, they'll need to recharge. Save them a fortune from using the hotel mini-bar and pack:

- Bottled water
- Snacks such as peanuts, crackers, and granola bars
- Some fruit

For an extra touch of comfort, you can add:

- A scented candle and matches
- Bath bubbles or salts
- Ear plugs and an eye mask

Or get creative and give them some things that can help them get around town a little more easily:

- A town map or guidebook
- A list of good restaurants and things to do in the area
- A subway card, loaded with fare money
- A gift card for an ice cream cone or other nearby fun things
- A souvenir, like an "I ♥ NY" T-shirt

Or perhaps you want to put some wedding-themed stuff in there to get them excited for the big day:

- Wedding-bell–shaped chocolates or cookies
- Jordan almonds, a wedding classic
- Candy hearts

Or even make the next morning a little bit easier:

- Tylenol
- Gift card for a cup of coffee
- Gatorade

Whatever it is you decide for the gift baskets is totally fine. They can be really elegant and upscale or fun and whimsical. Again, this is not a necessity, but it's fun—and gets you in good with the out-of-townies. They can be a difficult crowd.

"My specialty is chocolate chip cookies, so I thought it'd be cute to bake chocolate chip cookies and hand them out as favors. I burnt two batches and later realized I didn't have enough counter space to cool forty dozen cookies. In the end, I gave half my guests store-bought cookies. Shhh. Don't tell anyone."

—Anonymous Bride

Extra-curricular Activities

Suggesting attractions. Guests really appreciate personal suggestions of restaurants, tourist attractions, and other fun stuff they can do to occupy the extra hours of their trip. This saves them a lot of hassle and shouldn't be too difficult for you to dash off since you know your area. You can also add this to your wedding website so out-of-towners can start planning their itinerary before they get into town. Just add a few links and you're done.

Planning an extra bash or two. If you've got just a few out-of-towners attending the wedding, consider inviting them to your rehearsal dinner. While it's not necessary or expected, it will really be appreciated so your guests won't be twiddling their thumbs in their hotel room cursing you under their breath about how they've got nothing to do after flying all this way just to see you. Now if you've got more than four or five people coming in, this may be cost prohibitive, but there are other ways to keep the out-of-townies happy. Bridal magazines will tell you to plan a party the day before the wedding—a backyard picnic or a pool party. If you can swing it without going crazy, great. It's idyllic and delightfully informal. But if you know you'll be going crazy that day with last minute fittings, manicures, or bachelorette party prepping, consider *suggesting* a group outing for the out-of-towners, something you won't be expected to show up to. For instance, if a lot of people are coming in with kids, organize a day at the science center or local zoo the day before the wedding. Tell them to have a fun day at the beach and point out where they can go for public access. People do know how to entertain themselves, but they just might need a little bit of reminding, and it will look like you made a huge effort.

Another common extra bash is the next-day brunch, where wedding guests can get together and laugh about who did the most enthusiastic Electric Slide the night before. Nope, this one's not necessary either. You can always use the excuse that you have an early flight to catch in the morning to get out of the extra expense. But sometimes the in-laws offer to pay for the brunch, or you can simply suggest that everyone meet at the hotel restaurant for breakfast and each pays his own way. It's totally up to you and whether you predict you'll want your wedding weekend over fast or if you'll want to savor your out-of-towners' last moments with you while simultaneously savoring a few mimosas. There are no wrong answers here.

THE LOGISTICAL NIGHTMARE THAT IS YOUR SEATING CHART

Putting together a seating chart is like putting together a jigsaw puzzle, but not your ordinary jigsaw puzzle. This is one of those massive 3-D puzzles with over 1,000 pieces, all colored white. I almost had a nervous breakdown trying to get the seating chart to make sense at my wedding, and I'm supposed to be an expert. The thing is, you'll have all these wonderful groups of people RSVP to your wedding— your co-workers, your friends from yoga class, your in-laws and step-in-laws—but the number of people in each group will never equal the number of chairs that are placed at each table. Thus, the puzzle begins. Here are some strategies to solve it:

- Group people who know each other together. It might seem like a nice idea to mix them up and get them to mingle, but when it's time to sit down, they'll only have had a drink or two. Let them feel comfortable. People expect to socialize with others they know at dinner.
- "Head tables," where the bride and groom sit like a king and queen flanked by the bridesmaids and groomsmen, are okay, but they're becoming passé.

Let your wedding party sit with their dates and their friends at their own tables. You and the groom can sit at your own sweetheart table, or sit with your parents, his parents, or siblings.

- If your parents—or his (or both)—are divorced, create several VIP tables, separating the divorcees. Cluster these tables close to yours, in such a way that one doesn't seem more important than the rest. At each VIP table, you can seat a parent, his/her spouse and their close relatives, like your grandparents, uncles, aunts, and cousins on their side of the family. Group people together that make sense. Even if your divorced parents say they're calling a truce for the day, it's still awkward for everyone else at the table to have them sit together.

- If your parents have a couple friends who don't know anyone else there, you can put them at your parents' table, even if they're technically not VIPs. But if there isn't room for them, don't be afraid to put them somewhere else. They'll deal.

- Put college friends with other college friends, and work friends with other work friends, whether they're single or with dates. It's a nice idea to put all the single people together at one table, but they might feel like outcasts if all their pals are somewhere else—and they might be pissed thinking you were trying to fix them up with your gangly nineteen-year-old cousins.

- Seat young, sociable friends near the bar.

- Seat elderly relatives close to the buffet and away from speakers or sound systems.

- Whatever you do, don't tell anyone where they're sitting before the wedding; inevitably someone will want you to change your plans for them, and you shouldn't!

Unfortunately, the seating chart puzzle will never be perfect. You will make your best attempt at putting certain people together and separating others, but there still will be some timid cousins who have to sit next to your groom's gregarious—and inebriated—buddy from high school. There will be guests who feel slighted because they were seated too close to the door to the kitchen, and there will be a girlfriend from your sorority who was mad because all the cute guys were at a different table. There is no way to avoid this. Just do your best with the seating chart, try to make people happy, then *que sera sera*.

Or, you could consider letting everyone find their own seats at the reception. This is only recommended for a small reception, though. If you're having more than fifty people, waiting for everyone to play musical chairs could take all night.

TIMING IS EVERYTHING . . . ESPECIALLY ON YOUR WEDDING DAY!

The second logistical nightmare you're going to have to deal with is planning the wedding day itinerary. Yes, you already know what time the ceremony and the reception are going to start, and you probably have made a hair and makeup appointment, so you're pretty much done, right? Not necessarily. You still have got to figure out what time the photographer should show up, when your parents should show up, and when the groom and groomsmen need to get to the ceremony, making sure to stagger your schedules so you don't arrive at the exact same time, assuming you don't want to see each other before the ceremony.

This is where a wedding planner is infinitely valuable. This Type A nuptial guru will quickly zip off a list of who goes where and when, contact all vendors and tell them the plan, and make an itinerary for every man, woman, and flower girl in the wedding, complete with emergency phone numbers, and make sure the list is distributed. If you just gasped because you don't have a wedding planner and this sounds extremely necessary yet too scary to do on your own, never fear. You can actually hire a wedding planner to *just* do this part for you. You can even find a planner to show up on the big day to make sure it all goes according to plan—someone needs to bark orders at those groomsmen to whip them into shape! If a day-of planner is an option, maybe there's an ultra-organized friend (who isn't in the wedding party) who might be willing to be the go-to person for the organist/florist/groomsmen. You make the schedule and then pass it along to her. She can arrive an hour before the ceremony and be there to answer last minute questions, you know, the "Where is the bride's grandmother supposed to sit?" and "Where are the extra programs?" type crap.

Nervous about setting the schedule? Seems like a big job for one individual, eh? Don't worry, you can do this. Use the ceremony start time as a starting point and then work backwards. Figure out when you want the photographer to show up at your door—most brides want to be captured getting all gussied up in their gown. Then, work even further backwards to when you should hit the salon (if the hair and makeup people aren't coming to your house or hotel room). Your schedule might look something like this:

6:00 P.M. Ceremony start time

5:30 P.M. Bride, bridesmaids, and bride's family arrive at ceremony

5:15 P.M. Groom, groomsmen, and groom's family arrive at ceremony; photographer arrives to take pictures of them

4:50 P.M. Photographer leaves bride's house and drives to ceremony

3:50 P.M. Photographer arrives at bride's house to take pictures of bride, bridesmaids, and bride's family

3:30 P.M. Bride, bridesmaids, and bride's family all gather at the bride's house; snack

3:15 P.M. Bride and bridesmaids leave the hair salon

1:30 P.M. Hair appointments (this can vary depending on the number of bridesmaids, number of stylists, and hair design complexity)

1:15 P.M. Bride and bridesmaids arrive at hair salon

12:50 P.M. Leave lunch for the hair salon

12:00 P.M. Lunch

Don't use this schedule as gospel. Be sure you customize it completely to your own day, but yes, it will probably take you at least six hours to get ready for your wedding. If you're marrying at noon, I hope you're a morning person. As you plan, make sure you are realistic about how long each activity will take. If you're unsure, ask the appropriate vendor or wedding party member for an estimate.

Use your photographer as a resource. Photographers are used to documenting the whole day every step of the way. While I was creating my schedule, I found mine really helpful in suggesting the appropriate times for each activity.

Pad the schedule. If it normally takes fifteen minutes to get to your church, give yourself thirty. That way, if there's traffic or pictures take longer than you thought, you're covered. Think of worst-case scenarios for everything.

Pad the schedule even more. Operate under the notion that most people will arrive ten minutes late and most services will run ten minutes over schedule.

Think through the transportation. It can be especially challenging if you and your bridal party are separate from the groom and his party during the beginning of the day. If you've got a limo, it will have to transport you guys separately, and you'll have to allow extra time for the back and forth. If you want the wedding party to ride together to the reception, some people might have to leave their cars at the ceremony venue then go back to pick them up later on. Luckily, everyone will end up in the same place, so it will get figured out.

Hand out the itineraries to your groom, bridesmaids, parents, vendors, and whomever else will need to know where to be when. It's a great idea to highlight their need-to-know info, but give them the whole schedule so they can refer to it to find out where anyone else is at any given time. Also make a list of important cell phone numbers: your maid of honor's, your mom's, your dad's, your groom's, and your best man's. Leave yours off the list: have the maid of honor take frantic calls from florists and brides-maids with no sense of direction, so you can maintain your Chi.

HELLO, CHICKEN WITH ITS HEAD CUT OFF

I know this chapter is full of clichés, but the week before the wedding will truly be crazy in ways I cannot fully express without pulling out the overused headless poultry line. Suddenly, your wedding planner will be calling you wondering when you're going to bring the favors and decorations to the reception site, and you're going to be scrambling to get all the programs folded, picking up your dress from the seamstress, and fielding requests from long lost cousins about how they can spend some time with you while they're in town, even though you've got a wedding to finish planning. Oh, and you really need a manicure! How could you have forgotten to factor in time for that? There will inevitably be something you don't factor in. But you can get through it.

Take some extra vacation days. I know you're using the bulk of your vacation days for your honeymoon, but you might want to work over Thanksgiving and Christmas to accrue a few more pre-wedding days off work. Believe me, you'll be so relieved to have an extra sixteen hours or so. Of course, that's only if your boss is cool with you taking time off all at once.

Delegate wisely. Have your brother run the favors to the reception site and your mom pick up the programs at Kinko's, but be very specific with instructions. For example, your bro should see Pam in Event Coordination and leave the favors with her. You don't want the folks at the front desk munching on your candy favors because they think they were somehow a gift to them that magically got dropped off. Believe me, I've heard stranger!

Be thorough. While there are certain tasks that are okay to leave to others, there are a few that only you can do, like picking up your dress at the seamstress. This is because it's vitally important that you try on the dress and make sure it fits perfectly—and that you're happy with the alterations the seamstress has made. Also, be sure the dress is wrinkle-free, pin-free, and ready to wear.

> "Pack pliers in your emergency kit. I ended up needing them to squeeze the hooks that held up my train so it didn't keep falling down. A bridesmaid told me her friend used them to fix a clasp on the back of her dress. Pliers. On your wedding day. Who knew?"
>
> —Sarah

Avoid pre-partying. Yes, you will have guests in town and it will be tempting to go out to the bars with your old high school pals, and, of course, have some late night bachelorette-style revelry, but there is nothing that you'll regret more than a hangover on your wedding day. Being tired will make you cranky and long for your bed, rather than enjoy the fruits of your months of wedding planning labor.

No all-nighters either. You're wondering how you're going to get it all done, so you decide to stay up all night putting those guest giftbags together. Bad. Idea. If you really have to get it done, ask your teenage cousins to help out, or hire a concierge service to do the dirty work. This is the one time in your life you actually do need to play the beauty-rest card.

Just say no. Guests will call you with different requests throughout the week: "I know I said I didn't have a date but I just met this great guy on E-harmony. Can I bring him to the wedding?" or "Can we stop by for a quick visit before the rehearsal dinner—it's been so long since we saw you," or "I made streusel for you to have on the dessert table. Will you come over and pick it up?" Nicely tell them no. The head count for the venue was finalized already. Unfortunately, your schedule is too busy, but you're looking forward to seeing them at the wedding. And the streusel was such a lovely thought, but would they mind at all dropping them off for you, since your plate is very full right now?

Enlist your fiancé and a couple guys to handle deliveries to the reception venue. You'll probably have to get everything that's been taking up space in your home to the venue in advance of the wedding date. Usually it will be a day or two in advance so they don't have to store them too long, but early enough so they're there with plenty of time for staff to organize and set them up. This is a great job for that great guy of yours.

Make sure everything's labeled with your name and wedding date on it so the chances of it mysteriously going missing are lower. In Pittsburgh, it's a tradition to have a buffet of homemade cookies at your wedding—seriously, this is a real thing; the *New York Times* even did a story on it. One venue even has a "cookie contract" so that the site is not held liable for missing cookies on the wedding day. Yes, they are afraid of getting sued over cookies, and yes, it's likely things will go missing, so label, label, label.

Put your maid of honor or another trusted friend in charge of "the emergency kit." This is a large bag of helpful just-in-case junk that she'll embarrassed to have to haul around on the wedding day, but having it will make you feel infinitely better. Give her this list of items to pack:

- Hairspray
- Clear nail polish
- Double-sided hem tape
- Bandages
- Extra pair of pantyhose, if you're wearing them
- Sewing kit with thread to match your dress, the bridesmaids' dresses, and the guys' suits
- White chalk (to cover scuffs or smudges on your shoes or dress)
- Pain reliever
- Antacid
- Tweezers
- Nail file
- Nail clippers
- Scissors
- Hand lotion
- Lip balm
- Bobby pins
- Safety pins
- Makeup (to match what you'll have on)
- Blotting papers
- Translucent powder
- Tissues
- Comb
- Ponytail holders
- Deodorant

- Mints
- Breath spray
- Extra pair of contact lenses, if you wear them
- Saline solution

You never know what suckage might go down on the big day, so you might as well be prepared for anything.

As you're running around like a chicken with its head cut off, imagine that beach escape of a honeymoon that you have planned. That's liable to make you feel better. Didn't plan a honeymoon that will be wholly relaxing? Try to get in touch with your travel agent to change the plan. Now.

Chapter 11

Your Big Day (I Guess It's His Day Too)

It's finally here! Your wedding day! What had once seemed so far off in the distant future is now at your doorstep! But instead of being that poised, together, organized bride you had hoped to be, you're exhausted from running errands and pissed that your cake baker still hasn't called you back about what time your dessert will be delivered. Frustrated, you look at your hands and see little bitten nail nubs instead of that lovely French manicure you had hoped for. And you're distraught that instead of having a glowing, flawless complexion, your face is broken out and itchy with hives because you've been so anxious.

What's more is that even with all the months of painstaking planning and endless to-do lists, things could still go wrong. You could get stood up by any one of your vendors, your limo driver could get lost despite his assurance that he knows exactly where your street is, or your maid of honor could spill bleach on her dress the night before and call you crying in despair. And those are only the things you planned for!

But, goddamn it, this is the one day of your life that your friends and family will come together to celebrate

207

your marriage. The one day that you'll vow to spend the rest of your life with the man you love. And the one day that you'll be photographed more often than Tiger Woods during his sex scandal. So you have to figure out a way to put things in perspective and enjoy every last moment of it, no matter how imperfect it may be.

STARTING OFF ON THE RIGHT PEDICURED FOOT

Even if you've heeded my warnings and tucked yourself into bed at a decent hour with little to no alcohol coursing through your veins, you still might not get eight hours of beauty sleep. You may toss and turn worrying about missing bridesmaids or a catastrophic bad hair day. But no matter how many hours you slept, when you wake you need to start your day off on the right foot as best you can. Once your day gets going, you'll need to be at your best in order to deal with the unexpected. Because of this, I recommend:

Sticking to your usual morning routine. Get up at the regular time. If you normally run or do yoga in the morning, don't skip it. If you're like me and you hazily stumble over to the coffee maker first thing, have your normal amount of java. As much as you might want to do something different and special, give your body what it's used to so it will be at its optimum performance level.

Eating a good breakfast. Good=healthy. Give yourself some protein and some carbs for energy. On big days, I like to have some eggs, wheat toast, fruit, and juice or some other hearty, delicious balanced combo. Skip the bacon and sausage though. Greasy stuff will weigh you down and make you feel a bit like a sausage yourself when you try to squeeze into your Spanx.

Skipping the congregation. Plan on some quiet time alone in the A.M. If you have roommates or you live with your guy or you're staying with your parents, it's okay to spend the morning with the peeps in your house, but don't invite the neighborhood over for breakfast. You'll have enough people surrounding you for the rest of the day. Enjoy a little "you time" while you can.

> "A friend of my family had a $1,200 chapel length Monique Lhuillier veil and her new cat attacked it like a scratching post while it was on her head. She had to cut it the day of her wedding. Disaster!"
>
> —Emily

Packing snacks—and scheduling time to eat them. I know I've continually advised you to eat so you don't have a meltdown, but seriously, many brides forget to keep themselves fed throughout the wedding day—or decide not to eat because they think it will make them look skinnier (it won't). Low blood sugar = crankiness. So have good, healthy foods around you throughout the day. And don't skip lunch.

Pre-game lightly. Don't start drinking too early in the day. It might sound like fun to have tequila shots with the girls at lunch, but you're going to be greeting guests and making speeches—while surrounded by alcohol—all day long. This is a marathon, not a sprint, lady! So go ahead and have one glass of pre-ceremony champagne in the bride's room. Then save the rest of the alcohol for the reception.

MURPHY'S LAW-FULLY WEDDED BRIDE

After all the time, energy, money, and sacrifices you've made, you no doubt want your day to go exactly as planned. And that's fine, as long as your realize that it probably won't. You may have played out a million "what ifs" in your mind, but when things actually go wrong on your big day, it's bound to throw you for a loop. Fender benders, forgotten rings, drunk guests, bridesmaid in labor, MIA officiants, red wine spilt on a bride's dress—I've heard every wedding horror story there is. In these scenarios, even the most rational, level-headed bride will want to throw a tantrum, cry, or worse, internalize her feelings and let them ruin her enjoyment of the rest of the day. In order to avoid this, try:

Laughing. Okay, so say you put on your shoes and realize they've been mismarked and are actually three sizes too big. Before you freak out, think hard. This is hilarious—you're getting married in clown shoes! Giggle, dance around, put them on your flower girl, and laugh some more about how gigantic they are. Then, stick some cotton balls in the toes or borrow the maid of honor's heels. If you can laugh, you'll show true grace under pressure. And really, what will flipping out solve?

Understanding. Your groom left the rings at the hotel? This is not the time to lecture him and complain that if he's going to neglect to do this one important duty properly, what else is he going to neglect throughout your years of marriage? He's so irresponsible! Or is he? Try to remember, everyone else—especially the groom—is nervous and overwhelmed today too and messing up something like this doesn't mean he's an asshole, it just means he's human. Find a plan B, like borrowing your parents' rings for the ceremony, and move on.

Assigning. So the ceremony programs were accidentally delivered to the reception venue and they need to get to the synagogue. Don't let this weight get thrown on your shoulders. Instead, remember that in an emergency, you're supposed to point to one particular person and ask them to call 911. Pick your person—wedding planner, maid of honor, trusted friend, whomever it may be—and point. Say, "You're in charge of getting the programs and bringing them to the synagogue. Stat!" And consider it done.

Ignoring. I never in a million years expected my florist to show up on my wedding day with teeny tiny bridesmaid bouquets and a flower girl basket full of pink petals (even though I asked for white). When I saw them, I froze. My mom made some negative comments. Knowing that it was too late to have the florist change anything, I acknowledged that the bouquets and basket existed, then handed them out to my wedding party. I figured, why freak out when everyone was about to head down the aisle? The florist can have a piece of your mind after the wedding day (and you might be able to get some of your money back). For now, get those girls a-walkin'.

Venting. If something is really bothering you, such as Bridesmaid #4 showing up with a much, er, smaller dress than the one that was ordered for her, take a step back. Is she guilty of "slutting up" her dress? If you're not a hold-it-in kind of person and you feel you absolutely have to say something or you'll explode, pull aside your mom or another friend. Complain. Let it all out (as long as no one else can hear you) and move on with the rest of your day. Resist the urge to verbally abuse Ms. Sluts-a-lot. She's not making anyone look bad but herself.

Plan B-ing. One of the worst disasters that can happen on the wedding day is to hate your hairstyle or your makeup. It might sound vain, but if you don't feel comfortable with the way you look, you won't feel confident being in the spotlight. Every woman has a very stylish friend. Make sure yours is on speed dial in case of a hair or makeup emergency. I'm sure she'll be fully equipped to save the day.

"Nobody tells you that once you get in the dress you can't pee for hours unless someone lifts it up for you. Nobody tells you that you spend all this money on a cake to only get to taste it when your new hubby mashes it into your face. Or that when you get back to your hotel room after everything is over, that the two of you are too tired to even move."

—Christine

This is your one chance—your one day, no matter how many mistakes, screwed up hairdos, embarrassing sweat stains, and ugly decorations happen. If you let things that are beyond your control bother you, you'll truly be missing out. So take a deep breath and enjoy it, in all its imperfect glory.

BRIDAL BARBIE NEVER HAD TO DEAL WITH THIS CRAP

I remember putting on the dress and the veil and having my hair and makeup all done and looking in the mirror and saying, dumbfoundedly, "I look . . . like a bride!" I'm sure my bridesmaids had to resist the urge to say, "No shit." Be prepared. It can be a shock the first time you see yourself, and being a bride may not be a role you feel comfortable playing. How do you know how to do it? How do you enjoy the day while being a good host? How do you revel in being the center of attention while giving your groom the attention he deserves as well? How do you avoid being one of those women who barely even remembers her wedding day because it goes by in a blur? There are no right or wrong answers to these questions, but there is some advice:

Make an Energized Entrance

Walking down the aisle is your big moment. It's your time to shine, and most brides truly do. But occasionally, I'll be at a wedding and the bride will look like she's nervously walking down a plank rather than breezing down the aisle. That's because, unless you're a professional model who's comfortable strutting a catwalk, there is no way to practice for this event. One moment, you're safely behind double doors secure next to your dad or mom, and the next moment, all the eyes of everyone you've ever known are fixed on you while flashes are going off left and right. If you're the least bit shy or just happen to be a bundle of nerves on that day, it can be very uncomfortable, and unfortunately your discomfort could be mistaken for uneasiness about getting married and subsequently documented with eighty-seven point-and-shoot digital cameras.

Before you walk down the aisle, relax. Chat with Dad and Mom. Crack a joke. Reminisce with your maid of honor about the time you egged your math teacher's house. Take a deep breath and then walk. As you're walking, make eye contact with your groom and think about how happy you are that you're marrying him. It will show on your face—and help ease everyone's nerves, since no one likes to see an uneasy bride.

Remind Yourself to Remember

I hear time and time again from people that their memories of their wedding day are hazy. You're so busy getting pulled in different directions by your photographer who wants you to pose for yet another picture, by your mom who wants you to say hello to her friends from college, and by the guests who all vie for your attention. While this sounds kind of lame, it actually works: each time you find yourself really enjoying a once-in-a-lifetime moment, make the decision to enjoy it and remember enjoying it. As long as you're self aware—fully caffeinated and not yet drunk—you'll be sure to remember it.

Greet Guests Graciously

It goes without saying that you should be nice to your guests and thank them for attending your wedding, but you may not always get the chance to do so. In order to insure it, you can do a traditional receiving line where you and your groom line up near the exit at the ceremony site to connect with each guest. Everyone gets a personal greeting, and you won't feel like you have to race around at the reception to get to everyone. People love the receiving line, even though it's time consuming, contrived, and honestly, a real pain for you. The great thing about it, however, is that no one will complain that they came to your wedding and never even got to talk to you.

If there's no good space for you to create a receiving line or you'll have so many guests that it's just not feasible, consider some other plan to greet everyone. My husband and I decided we wanted to walk around to each of the tables after dinner. However, what we didn't realize is that people try to have long conversations with you when there isn't a line full of people behind them as motivation to hustle along. We made it to exactly two tables before we got whisked off to cut the cake. If this happens to you, don't beat yourself up about it. Hit the dance floor and have fun.

Do What Makes You Comfortable

If you hate being the center of attention, you might be dreading the wedding day. Plan to make yourself as comfortable as possible by not putting too much pressure on yourself. If you feel nervous speaking in front of crowds, don't make a fancy speech—leave those up to the maid of honor, the best man, and your dad. If you're stressed out thinking you'll look like a fool during the first dance, have the DJ invite other couples onto the dance floor to share it with you too. Don't do anything out of your comfort zone and you'll feel a lot less stress on your wedding day.

Avoid Over-Scheduling

I thought I wanted my photographer to capture a million group shots with different segments of our families and groups of friends, so we took some time out of the reception and gathered in the hotel lobby for pics. The problem was, while my husband and I waited for each group to arrive for their photo, we were missing the party that was going on. It wasn't worth it! While we do have a lot of family photos (most of which look the same), we sacrificed a lot of memories. I've seen some couples have the entire wedding party gather for a massive group shot, or provide a photo booth so people can have their own picture taken at their leisure. These are much better ideas than what we did.

Live in the Moment

Too many brides spend their wedding day worrying about whether everyone else is having a good time and forget to have a good time themselves. So enjoy yourself! You're not on a diet anymore, so have some stuffed mushroom appetizers and a giant piece of cake. Maybe you want to act prim and proper during the ceremony, but it's okay to let loose at the reception. If you want to have a cake fight with your fiancé or jump into the pool fully clothed with your bridesmaids, go ahead and do it. Don't let anyone tell you it's uncouth or immature if this is something you'll feel good doing.

Don't Get Drunk—Until the Very End

I know I mentioned this before, but it's not a good idea to get drunk. You'll be nervous and it will be easy to let the wine flow faster than usual, so this will take a concerted effort on your part. Alternate alcoholic beverages with several glasses of water or seltzer (this will also keep you hydrated as you get down on the dance floor), and stick with wine or a weak cocktail rather than martinis or anything with "just a splash of" soda.

If you really want to get tipsy on your wedding day, wait until after all the toasts and opportunities for public speaking—and public embarrassment—are over. This might mean limiting it to only a drink or two until the after-party. Or you can hold out for the bottle of champagne you have stashed on ice in the bridal suite.

Oh, and P.S.: never drink out of a brown beer bottle in a wedding dress—it looks unbelievably tacky in the photos, and you'll definitely regret it.

Have Alone Time with Your Groom

Reminder: As much fun as it is to share this day with everyone else in your life, it truly is about you and your groom. So at some point in the day, be sure to spend just a little bit of alone time with your new husband—don't let it wait until the very end.

"Our wedding was a disaster on so many levels. The bridesmaids' dresses got lost, I fainted on the altar, one guest got in a car crash in the parking lot, and the band was horrible—and that's not even the half of it! But the objective that day was to get married, and we did. We've been married for over thirty years now."

—Jane

The Jewish culture has a lovely tradition called *Yichud*, in which the bride and groom steal away for a little while right after the ceremony. These first moments as husband and wife are spent undistracted by other people—

I'm guessing that at one time the reason for this tradition might have been to consummate the marriage right then and there, but today it's just about the newly married couple finding some peaceful togetherness. It doesn't matter what your culture, you can adopt this idea and make it your own.

If you can't make it happen right after the ceremony, sit at a sweetheart table for two at the reception, or simply grab him at some point during the reception and talk about how happy you are to be married to him. Perhaps watch the sunset together while your photographer takes your picture. Or take one last slow dance together in the hotel room after the reception has ended. Whatever it is, look into his eyes and enjoy the moment.

Stay Grounded

During your wedding, you're like queen for a day—at least the beginning part, when bridesmaids are lifting your train and holding your purse for you. But by the time your dress gets bustled and your clutch finds its way to your dinner table, everyone will be attending the party and not really tending to *you*. And that's okay. Your handmaidens deserve to have fun at your wedding and, except for when you need them to lift your ball gown so you can pee, should be left alone to enjoy themselves. So quit barking orders and let your friends enjoy the party.

Play the Escape By Ear

Some couples plan to make a grand exit through a shower of confetti and hop into a getaway car, waving to guests as they drive off. Others stay until the very last song has been played and every last guest has headed out the door. I actually like the idea of playing the exit by ear. You two might feel totally energized and join everyone at the hotel bar for an after-party, or you might start feeling frisky and secretly slink out the door together without so much as an adios to the crowd. Your mood and how the reception unfolds is a better way to gauge what's best for you, so don't have it writ in stone. Yes, I finally told you *not* to plan something!

Conclusion

THE HONEYMOON'S OVER ... LITERALLY

You're home from your exotic vacation, hopefully more in love than you could have possibly imagined. Your husband (it still feels weird to call him that!) carries you over the threshold to symbolize starting your lives together as husband and wife. Now, as you gaze at the proofs the photographer sent, your wedding feels like eons ago instead of a just a couple of weeks past. Looking back, you realize all the stress, outbursts, crying spells, and binge drinking were all for nothing. Your wedding turned out to be a huge success! Not because the flowers were spectacular or the bridesmaids' dresses fit perfectly or the cake was moist or the band was kick-ass, but because your wedding did exactly what it was supposed to do: transition you from being engaged to being a married couple! So what if the baker sent you the "Happy Bar Mitzvah" cake by mistake or your mother-in-law objected when the priest asked guests to "speak now or forever hold your peace." You'll laugh about those things in the days to come (okay, maybe it will take years for the mother-in-law thing!). I love that I had to take the subway to my wedding and that my groom turned to his best man to have breath spray squirted in his mouth before the big kiss on the altar. I don't love the fact that some friends got plastered playing beer pong in their hotel rooms afterwards and caused other hotel guests to complain to the front desk, but I can laugh about it now. And I don't love that I rarely talk to one of my former bridesmaids, but at least the wedding taught me who my friends, in fact, are.

I guess what I'm saying is that no matter what type of events happened at your wedding, both sucky and sensational, that the wedding belonged to you and your man.

Your very own once-in-a-lifetime wedding where you and the man of your dreams promised to love, honor, and cherish each other. So go ahead and do just that! If you survived the turmoil of wedding planning, overcoming marriage issues like sharing closet space and finding empty milk containers in the fridge will be a walk in the park. In fact, maybe that's the point of having a wedding after all. It's sort of a litmus test for marriage. And since you passed the test with flying colors, I'm sure you'll have a wonderful life filled with oodles of anniversaries and grandchildren. And so I offer to you both my sincerest wishes for a long, healthy, and happy life together.

Resource Section

Resource Section

GENERAL WEDDING PLANNING

There are some good websites you can visit for lots of general wedding planning information, such as how-to articles and photo galleries of gowns. They include:

Brides.com. This is the website for *Brides* magazine, but there are also archives of articles that ran in now-defunct *Modern Bride* and *Elegant Bride*, so there's lots of information available here.

TheKnot.com. This is a one-stop shop for wedding planning information. Not only does the site have lots of how-to articles, it also has tools to help you out, like a budget worksheet that calculates your spending for you, and a planning checklist. You can also create your own wedding website there. Some brides also love their online community, where you can commiserate with other brides going through the same stuff as you are.

BridalGuide.com. This one isn't as extensive as the previous two, but it has a bunch of articles I wrote while I was a staffer there, so if there's anything I know about wedding planning that I haven't told you in this book, it's probably there.

WeddingWire.com. A site that lists local vendors—and has starred reviews—and also has active forums.

Weddings.About.com. It's got good how-to style articles on lots of aspects of wedding planning.

Weddings.iVillage.com. This women's website thoroughly covers a wide variety of topics, one of which is weddings. It has plenty of planning articles—there's even a whole section on handling stress—and a cool tool that helps you find your dream dress.

WEDDING TALK AND INSPIRATION

Stylemepretty.com. A photo-heavy blog that's full of photos of amazing real weddings and other aesthetic ideas.

WeddingBee.com. Follow other brides as they blog their way through wedding planning.

VENDORS AND SERVICES

If you're looking for a vendor and you don't have any recommendations from family and friends, Google will probably yield way too many results—most of which you know nothing about. Instead, you might want to start with a site that has user reviews, such as:

Yelp.com

CitySearch.com

WeddingWire.com

If your area has a local site with reviews, that's a good place to go, too.

Unsure of a wedding vendor? Check out:

The Better Business Bureau. Go to bbb.org to find your local office and give them a call, or search their online database for any complaints from consumers who've used the vendor's services.

Wedding Planners

For wedding professionals, it's often a good indication if they're involved in some sort of industry organization because they've learned many tricks of the trade from others in the industry and they answer to certain standards. There are several associations for wedding planners, but I like The Association of Bridal Consultants, BridalAssn.com.

Stationery

Some of my favorite wedding invitation designers and sellers include:

WeddingPaperDivas.com. Cool, modern invites by different designers; from casual to traditional and elegant, they run the gamut.

Crane.com. Crane & Co. offers gorgeous engraved and thermographed invites printed on high-end papers.

CatSeto.com. A designer who creates vintage-style stationery with updated whimsy. (And she's really nice too!) Some styles are adorned with crystals.

Target.com. Check out their DIY invitation kits.

FineStationery.com. A site that's culled from the work of many different designers. There's plenty to choose from here. Even if you're not buying online, you can go here for invitation inspiration.

HelloLucky.com. These letterpress designers are amazing! See for yourself. You can have them design all your wedding stationery from scratch or choose from many pre-made motifs. If letterpress printing is out of your price range, they offer digital as well.

For help with invitation wording and etiquette, go to VerseIt.com.

Create Your Own Wedding Website
Do it for free or a small fee at:

TheKnot.com

WeddingChannel.com

eWedding.com

OneWed.com

Webs.com

Wedding Favors
You can always troll the stores for favor ideas, but starting online is a good idea. (You don't have to buy online though. Case in point: you see cute chocolates on a website and have a local chocolate shop whip up something similar instead.) On the web, I like these sources for wedding favors that are affordable and unique:

Beau-coup.com. My go-to site for wedding favors. They've got everything from the items themselves (customized cookies) to the packaging (boxes and ribbons in your colors and custom-printed tags).

WeddingFavorites.com. They've got some nice favors with modern tags and color schemes. Eco-friendly favors, too.

WeddingThings.com. This is up there with Beau-coup and WeddingFavorites. The site has so many things to choose from. Definitely go there if you're stumped and need ideas.

Party Decorations and Wedding Extras

To make your pre-party and reception décor complete, check out these sites for supplies:

EstiloWeddings.com. Elegant table number and place card ideas that will wow guests.

PlumParty.com. For a more casual bash, check out this site's themed stuff (motifs range from casino to lobsters to wine). It also has some cute favor ideas.

PearlRiver.com. The go-to place for everything Asian-inspired: paper lanterns to hang at the reception, paper fans to keep guests cool at an outdoor ceremony, and parasols for the bridesmaids. They're very affordable too.

ForYourParty.com. If you want stuff personalized, go here. Napkins, matchbooks, coasters, menus, programs, and more. And they're not super cheesy either.

Floral Props

For affordable vases, ribbons, votive candles, and more, try:

IKEA

Michael's

AC Moore

Jo-Ann Fabrics

Photography and Videography Associations

If you're having trouble finding a photo or video pro near you, maybe one of these organizations can help:

Wedding & Event Videographers Association International, WEVA.com

Wedding Photojournalist Association, WPJA.com

International Society of Professional Wedding Photographers, ISPWP.com

Reception
iPod DJing: If you have been living under a brick and haven't done so already, go to Apple.com/iTunes and download iTunes. With it, you can buy almost any song you could possibly want. Oh, and you should have an iPod or other MP3 player, and access to a good speaker system, too. Your site may have speakers you can rent or suggestions for where you can get them.

Portable Restrooms: Check with local rental companies to see what they offer. These portable bathrooms are kind of like trailers and can range from bare-bones to luxurious.

Kohler, the upscale bathroom fixture company, also rents out "luxury bathroom trailers." Sounds like an oxymoron, but they're actually pretty nice-looking. Check out KohlerPower.com.

Guest List and Other Etiquette Help
Emily Post's Etiquette by Peggy Post
Emily Post's Wedding Etiquette by Peggy Post

NONTRADITIONAL WEDDING REGISTRIES

REI.com

Traveler's Joy Honeymoon Registry, Travelersjoy.com

Target.com

Amazon.com's wedding registry

FITNESS RESOURCES

Need help getting in shape for the big day? Check out:

BootCampFinder.com. Search for a boot camp program near you.

ACEFitness.com. ACE-certified personal trainer search engine.

BridalBootcampOnline.com. A subscription-only website that helps you create your own boot camp routine.

Women's Health: The Wedding Workout—it gets good reviews on Amazon.

Dieting Sucks by Joanne Kimes
iTunes—look for free fitness podcasts!

Craigslist.org—look for free fitness classes in your area
Wii Fit

BEAUTY REFERENCE AND IDEAS

DailyGlow.com

Sephora: The Ultimate Guide to Makeup, Skin, and Hair from the Beauty Authority by Melissa Schweiger

iVillage.com/beauty

BellaSugar.com

InStyle.com

Beauty Products

Read reviews of items at these sites. Most will let you return the product if it's the wrong color, so you don't have to be afraid to buy online.

Sephora.com

Drugstore.com

Beauty.com

BigelowChemists.com

Teeth whitening
BriteSmile.com

ZoomNow.com

Crest White Strips, available at Amazon.com, Drugstore .com, or your local drugstore

Colgate Total Advanced Whitening toothpaste, Colgate .com

Spas and Massage Therapists
Find a good spa or independent massage pro at:

SpaFinder.com
American Massage Therapy Association

Microdermabrasion: Here are some products you can try at home to get smooth, more even-toned skin:

Mary Kay TimeWise Microdermabrasion Kit, MaryKay .com

Philosophy, The Microdelivery, Micro-Massage Exfoliating Wash

Hair Removal
Some popular products: Zip Wax, hot wax hair remover, Drugstore.com

RELATIONSHIPS/MARRIAGE/LIVING TOGETHER

TheFrisky.com

TheNest.com

YourTango.com

The Good Girl's Guide to Living in Sin: The New Rules for Moving In With Your Man by Joselin Linder and Elena Donovan Mauer

Engaged and Married Sex

Have Sex Like You Just Met . . . No Matter How Long You've Been Together: Every Girl's Guide to a Sexy and Satisfying Relationship by Joselin Linder and Elena Donovan Mauer

Sex: How to Do Everything by Em and Lo

SheKnows.com Presents: The Best Sex of Your Life, 101 Secrets Every Woman Should Know by Jennifer Hunt and Dan Baritchi

TRAVEL TIPS

Be sure to plan ahead for your honeymoon or destination wedding.

Check out vaccination requirements and recommendations at cdc.gov/travel. Then make an appointment to see your doctor to get your shots/malaria meds.

Be sure your driver's licenses, passports, and visas are all up-to-date.

Index

About the Authors

Elena Donovan Mauer is a former editor at *Bridal Guide* and *Modern Bride* magazines, where she ate (yup, free cake samples!), wrote, and (practically) breathed weddings. She's also written for TheKnot.com, WeddingBee.com, and Brides.com. She's had two weddings—in which she married the same groom, Anthony. One ceremony was intimate City Hall nuptials attended by only their very nearest and dearest. The other was a traditional church ceremony followed by a 200-person bash. Seven years later, Elena and Anthony have finally recovered from the suckiness of wedding planning and live in New Jersey with their son. Elena is also the coauthor of *The Good Girl's Guide to Living in Sin* and *Have Sex Like You Just Met . . . No Matter How Long You've Been Together*, both published by Adams Media.

Joanne Kimes is the creator of the Sucks series, whose titles include: *Dating Sucks, Dieting Sucks, Pregnancy Sucks, Pregnancy Sucks for Men, Divorce Sucks, Teenagers Suck, Breastfeeding Sucks*, and many others. She has also written for several children's television shows including *Roundhouse* and *Sweet Valley High* and has penned numerous articles for magazines and websites. When planning her own wedding, she and her fiancé got so overwhelmed that they canceled everything and ran off and eloped. To this day, they don't regret their decision.

Getting Where Women Really Belong

- Trying to lose the losers you've been dating?
- Striving to find the time to be a doting mother, dedicated employee, and still be a hot piece of you-know-what in the bedroom?
- Been in a comfortable relationship that's becoming, well, too comfortable?

Don't despair! Visit the Jane on Top blog—your new source for information (and commiseration) on all things relationships, sex, and the juggling act that is being a modern gal.

Sign up for our newsletter at
www.adamsmedia.com/blog/relationships
and download a **Month-ful of Happiness!**
That's 30 days of free tips guaranteed to lift your mood!